ALSO BY LILLIAN ROSS

Picture

Portrait of Hemingway

Moments with Chaplin

The Player

Vertical and Horizontal

Reporting

Talk Stories

Takes

HERE
BUT NOT
HERE

HERE BUT NOT HERE

A Love Story

LILLIAN ROSS

RANDOM HOUSE
NEW YORK

 Published in the United States by Random House, Inc., New York, and simultaneously in Canada by Random House of Canada Limited, Toronto.

Grateful acknowledgment is made to *The New Yorker* for permission to use the following materials: quote from a note from Don Wharton dated August 30, 1934; excerpt from a letter from Katharine White to Lillian Ross dated June 27, 1949; excerpt from Harold Ross's notes dated October 10, 1949; excerpt from a letter from Harold Ross to Lillian Ross dated August 1, 1950; excerpt from William Shawn's letters to the staff of *The New Yorker* from Fall, 1976; William Shawn's special message to advertisers dated December 11, 1978; William Shawn's "Notes and Comments" from the April 22, 1985, issue of *The New Yorker;* William Shawn's farewell letter dated February 12, 1987, and excerpts from William Shawn's story "The Catastrophe" from the November 14, 1936, issue of *The New Yorker.* All material used here by permission of *The New Yorker.*

Library of Congress Cataloging-in-Publication Data
Ross, Lillian
Here but not here / Lillian Ross.
p. cm.
ISBN 0-375-50119-3
1. Ross, Lillian. 2. Shawn, William. 3. *New Yorker* (New York, N.Y. : 1925) 4. Women journalists—United States—Biography. 5. Periodical editors—United States—Biography.
I. Title.
PN4874.R62A3 1998 070'.92—dc21
[B] 97-43669

Random House Website address: www.randomhouse.com
Printed in the United States of America on acid-free paper
2 4 6 8 9 7 5 3
First Edition

Book design by J. K. Lambert

TO WILLIAM SHAWN

ACKNOWLEDGMENTS

In 1993, Katrina Heron, a young *New Yorker* editor with whom I was working on a piece for the magazine, suggested that I might try to write about my life with William Shawn. She was the first to lend her wisdom and her expertise to the creation of this book. Also embedded in my writing are the considerable talents of Sharon DeLano and Jeffrey Frank, who contributed to the early shaping of the story. I thank them for their ingenious work. I'm indebted to Tina Brown for her unwavering encouragement, her moral support, her creative participation, and, most of all, for her cheerful understanding of love.

I'm grateful to my Random House master editor, Kate Medina, her alert and multitalented assistant, Meaghan Rady, and copy editor Virginia Avery, for helping to bring me from the story to the book. And I thank Sarah Harrison Smith for her reassuring touches in the cause of accuracy.

George Sheanshang, Peter Parcher, and Amy Gutman gave me invaluable guidance for the book, and from start to finish, my patient and accomplished agent, Jane Gelfman, has been my loyal partisan.

I thank my son, Erik Ross, for his practical help with the computer, his sensitive editorial judgment, his keen memory, and his incredible and beloved presence.

CONTENTS

HERE BUT NOT HERE

CHAPTER 1

AS WE WERE

All enduring love between two people, however startling or unconventional, feels unalterable, predestined, compelling, and intrinsically normal to the couple immersed in it, so I would have to say that I had an intrinsically normal life for over four decades with William Shawn, the late editor of *The New Yorker*. We loved each other. We remained in love with each other until the day he died, unexpectedly, on December 8, 1992. We signed off every telephone call, every casual parting, every "good night"—including that of the night before his death—with "I love you." From the first instance of his open declaration of love, Bill Shawn continued to say it and to make me feel his love. I learned to respond with the same word. "Love" isn't a word I take lightly or tire of today.

My life became both turbulent and magical as it changed from my initial role as a single-minded reporter and writer into what became everything else I was alive for. I started out seemingly unsuited to be entrusted with my additional role. But I wound up possessing it, and with it, I was given the greatest satisfaction I know of. I have a lasting sense of the normalcy of it all. It was a normalcy that Bill Shawn was able to create for himself and for me against all normal odds.

Our life together did not feel ordinary, however. Bill Shawn was incapable of engaging in the ordinary. He was incapable of imagining the ordinary, whether he was composing a passage to be incorporated into a writer's story for *The New Yorker*, or a gift card, or a poem, or a letter of love. He was deeply romantic, and in giving voice to his feelings in traditional ways, he managed to say "I love you" so that it sounded fresh. He was my steady collaborator, both personally, in the life we made together, and professionally, from the time I was a young writer on his magazine. Since his death, my understanding of him and my wonder at him have broadened, and I find that our feelings for each other are still having their say. They touch and affect every aspect of my work and of my actions, including the telling of this story. I see it whole. And I see it in focus.

The scene is our living room:

It is a beautiful, mild, early September afternoon in 1987. Bill is in his seventies. I am in my sixties. He is quite bald, with a dark, substantial fringe of hair, carefully barbered, at the base of his skull. My hair is silver, curly, and cut short. We have similar faces—round, with high coloring. His eyes are pure light blue; mine are green. It is about six months after he left his job at *The New Yorker* and I went with him. We are in the apartment we found together about thirty years earlier, in a then brand-new building. It is on the twelfth floor; this had been our joint choice, notwithstanding his lifelong claustrophobia, his fear of heights, and his terror in most elevators. He lived "within limits," he would say. He had never been able to fly in a plane. On a highway, he once explained to me, he had to be sure there was an exit nearby. If he was caught in a traffic jam, he would grow silent and rigid. Once, when we were in a car, halted in bumper-to-bumper traffic on a road in New York City's Central Park, we had to get out and walk to the street. He would say he could not go outside in a heavy storm, rain or snow, or in a deep freeze. I discovered that he was able, surprisingly, to stretch his limits.

Our apartment is located about half a mile south of the one he lives in with his wife, Cecille. They were married in 1928, the day after he turned twenty-one. By 1958, when Bill and I chose this apartment, we had already been together, in other rooms, for several years. He and I had agreed we would not keep our liaison a secret from Cecille. When Bill told her about it, they talked for weeks, and then for months, with each other—an agonizing time for both of them—and then she made her unshakable decision: she would stay in the marriage, and he would make the logistical arrangements with her that our life together called for. Now, in 1987, Bill and Cecille have three grown children, and I have a son in his last year of college to whom, since his birth, Bill has been like a devoted parent. He has never considered divorcing his wife, and I have never considered asking him to. Whatever the circumstances in his marriage, Bill not only worried about Cecille, he loved her and would go on loving her, but he felt driven to make his life with me, and I have never doubted that this place has been our home.

Since we no longer have an office at *The New Yorker* to go to, we are spending a good deal of time together alone in the apartment. We have tried working in a nearby library and in a friend's office, but mostly we like being at home, which looks much the same as it has for years. Bill has always decorated our rooms, and I defer to him completely in matters of taste. Our first piece of furniture, a Danish teakwood rocking chair, is in this living room, which is large, sunny, bright, and simple, with picture windows at one end. We are looking out at a clear sky of pale blue, the color he loved. A beige-silk-upholstered sofa is against a wall, with lamps beside it.

A Steinway upright in ebony, with matching chair, stands against the opposite wall. Bill's brown leather briefcase, scuffed and bulging, rests, unopened, in a corner of the sofa. Bookshelves are filled with classics: Bill's favorites—Turgenev, Proust, Joyce, Jefferson, Fitzgerald, Shelley, Musil. My favorites include Gogol, Keats, Kafka, and Salinger. We have old-fashioned record albums along with CDs, and we play a lot of Duke Ellington, the Modern Jazz Quartet, and Mozart.

Between the books and the records stands a framed color photograph of Bill, taken in 1966, sitting on our sofa with his arm around my son, Erik, barefoot, at age five months; Bill is wearing tortoiseshell glasses, and he is reading *The New Yorker* to Erik. The photograph is one of the scores of photographs I've taken of them with a Leica Reflex camera given to me by Bill. Every time I pick up this camera, I think of how he said, as he handed it to me, that I should record for both of us what only I might see.

On the shelves are a few elegant items: an antique Chinese vase of a light shade of blue matching the color of Bill's eyes (he brought it back from a quick trip to Chicago, his hometown); a French porcelain teapot circa 1800 (one of his rare extravagances). A round dining table, covered with a white lacy cloth, is set with an English floral teapot and matching cups and saucers. Bill has always loved observing the custom of afternoon tea. Delicate Italian chairs of cherry wood and cane are at the table. The table's centerpiece is a basket of pale yellow tea roses, which Bill sends over regularly. Thirty-seven years earlier, he gave me similar flowers in a similar basket for the first time, saying that he wanted to call our friendship by its right name: love.

At that time, I found the flowers and what he said surprising and disconcerting. I found them frightening. I didn't want to recognize their meaning.

On this September afternoon in 1987, Bill is wearing a dark-blue cashmere suit with matching vest, a blue-and-white checked shirt, a dark-blue knitted tie. He is slightly built, high-complexioned, a bit paunchy around the middle, somewhat round-shouldered, and short (about five six), and he has big feet, encased in plain black shoes. Most of the time, whatever the season, he feels cold. On hot days, when most men are in shirtsleeves, he wears his usual warm dark-blue cashmere three-piece suit. About twenty years ago, he would wear a brown tweed suit, or a cotton seersucker suit in the heat of a New York summer, but now he stays with dark blue the year around. Outdoors, well before the onset of winter and into late spring, he wears a heavy alpaca-lined-and-collared coat, a muffler, and heavy gloves. Over his vest he wears a dark-green cashmere sleeveless sweater. He wears the same battered and soiled felt hat the year around, including steaming August days. (I gave the hat to him at least a dozen years earlier.)

The picture windows look out across a wide street to a red brick apartment house. Both of us like to look at what is going on in that house. Children are jumping on a bed in one apartment; in another, a fat black woman in a white uniform is sitting in a window, smoking a cigar; in still another, a middle-aged man in tights is doing aerobics in front of a television screen. A clock on a bookshelf near our piano indicates the time—almost four o'clock. It is the hour Bill loves. He calls it the hour of hope. For him, it conjures up romantically dressed and happy men, women, and children seated at a round table on a green lawn next to an English garden and having scones with large helpings of sweet butter and jam. We have gone often to the nearby Carlyle Hotel for afternoon tea, freshly brewed and served on English china, but we have not been able to conjure up any green lawn and garden there.

Bill sits down at the piano. I'm in our treasured rocking chair, wearing light-blue chambray jeans, a white tennis shirt, and sandals. I feel no need to dress up. Whatever I wear, I always feel his approval. I'm relaxed and comfortable, and I'm happy just looking at him. At this moment, everything in our room here feels right. I'm deeply aware, as always, of my own happiness to be with him. I don't take this moment for granted, perhaps because over the years we have had to face and conquer so many threats and challenges to our being together. At any rate, for more than half my life now, I have never taken our moments together for granted. Every time we are about to rejoin each other after having been apart—whether for a few minutes or a few hours or a few days—I'm aware of my eagerness to see him again, and I'm aware of how happy I feel every time I catch sight of him. From time to time, we compare notes with each other on this not-so-unusual shared manifestation, and neither one of us feels foolish expressing it. We've never wearied of trying out our thoughts on each other. This living room has been serene and beautiful for us, and I constantly feel privileged to be in it. In fact, every time I enter this room, I continue—to the present—to think of how Bill, on the day we moved in, brought flowers and said, "Blessings on this house."

Bill warms up at the piano by playing a little boogie-woogie. He plays by ear; he's never learned to read music. I go from the rocking chair to the sofa, the better to hear what he will do today. Abruptly, he stops playing. He turns to me.

He tells me that his feelings used to overwhelm him, and he couldn't talk, or say with his music what he felt. But now he feels free. Then he turns back to the piano and swings into his particular rendition of "In a Sentimental Mood," by Duke Ellington. Bill has told me that it was Ellington's own favorite song. We often play a recording of it, with John Coltrane on saxophone, that is, Bill says, the purist Ellington.

He has told me many things over the years about Ellington, including that he said, "If it sounds good, it is good." When Duke Ellington died, in 1973, Bill went to see him laid out at the Walter Cooke Funeral Home, located then at the corner of Third Avenue and East Eighty-fifth Street, a few blocks away from our apartment. He took me along and also my son, who was then seven years old. It was the first visit any of us had ever paid to a funeral home. We stood, silent and awed, for a long time, looking at Duke Ellington's body lying in a white satin-lined coffin and dressed in white tails. After that, we went home, where Bill sat down at the piano. Trying not to weep in front of the child, Bill played one Ellington number after the other—"In a Sentimental Mood," "Do Nothing Till You Hear from Me," "The Jeep Is Jumpin'," "Sophisticated Lady," "Tough Truckin'," "Prelude to a Kiss," and many others. Then, when Bill finally broke down and everybody was weeping, we played Ellington recordings very loudly for the entire evening.

Bill does not try to imitate Duke Ellington while playing the piano; he has his own style—hunched over the keyboard, rigid, almost tortured, hitting the piano keys and pumping the pedals vigorously. He looks very serious. He makes some mistakes and tightens up. He has strong hands, with long, tapered fingers and well-kept short fingernails. At the piano this afternoon, he pumps his feet energetically on the pedals. He starts playing Gershwin's "Someone to Watch Over Me," turning his head to look at me. We both smile. He turns to the piano again, looking somewhat absent. He stops playing and comes over and sits down next to me.

William Shawn was known to the world for half a century as the famous and revered editor of a famous and revered magazine. He was that, of course. To me, though, he became the man I loved, and a man whose individual, creative gifts were obscured and thwarted by his success. He was a tormented man, a man who had the desires of a poet but the duties of a caretaker, and of a muse, of poetics. By the time I met him, in 1945, when I began to write for *The New Yorker,* he had become responsible for the writers and artists around him, to the exclusion of his own creative impulses. He would often say that he felt he did not "exist." He felt eternally designated to serve others in their endeavors; at the same time he struggled to hold on to, as he put it, "a fading belief in my own reality." He was, in short, oddly cursed by his great gift for making it possible for others to communicate their art, for he was never able to give that gift to himself.

Almost anonymously, he poured his unique literary and comic gifts into the work of dozens of famous writers and artists, finding ways of concealing himself in them. His attentiveness to the needs of others went far beyond the concerns of a committed editor. For many people he came to represent all that defined a true and ideal editor. To me, he was a man who grieved over all living creatures but did not know how to grieve over himself, who seemed to know how to fight in behalf of others for the things they wanted or deserved but was baffled, and at times, wistful, about his inability to fight for himself.

He felt imprisoned by his job—he once described it to me as "the ultimate cell"—but he did not know how to fight free of it. Eventually, he spoke to me about himself with detachment and without self-indulgence. "Who has blotted me out?" he would ask softly and, it seemed to me, chillingly. In his face I saw a hunger for gaiety and humor. Seeing and sensing this, I didn't feel called upon at first to respond with anything beyond my writing; what I was in love with was reporting and writing. I could make him laugh with that. When I had written a story for him that I knew in my bones would delight him, his serious, youthful face would come alive, starting with stifled laughter that gradually broke out of control into a kind of apppreciative cry. That was enough for me. I didn't think I would be asked for anything more.

"I am there, but I am not there," Bill said over and over again, about his married life. The first time, early in the 1950s, that I heard this statement, I accepted it. He said he yearned for freedom, for fresh air, for lightheartedness, for warmth. I accepted his telling me that he felt enclosed, imprisoned, often intolerably, by his job, among other things. However, I found myself resisting the responsibility of understanding this. He wanted what he called a "sign" from somebody who might fight for his staying alive, for protecting him. He clutched tenaciously and desperately at that possibility. In his own way, he battled courageously for it, and yet he didn't know how to ask anyone for that "sign." Then he began to speak with abandon to me.

"I am there, but I am not there." I might wonder if this was the key to his entire being: his feeling of being enclosed, trapped. But how could I measure it? How could I judge it? It was what he said, what he was living. He never saw himself in a contradiction. It was *literally* the way he saw himself. I never doubted anything he told me. I was never a woman who arrogated to herself the right to analyze, to intrude upon, or to direct what another person was feeling. I never did that in my writing about people; I always wanted to trust the facts and let them reveal the truth. I accepted what Bill told me. His terror of imprisonment was like a waking nightmare.

In the beginning, I may have sensed his unspoken plea for release from his terror, but I did not understand it. Nor did I have to understand it. I was not looking for any emotional response other than to my writing. I wanted to keep my emotions focused on my writing. At *The New Yorker*, like the other staff members, I was engaged in creating stories that were mine and mine alone. My social life was mostly in a separate area, with other people, and I guarded my writing territory from all of that.

I did not know, before I found myself enmeshed—more and more deeply over the years—in a full life with Bill Shawn, where being loved by Bill Shawn would take me. There was never a blueprint. Where indeed it took me was unprecedented—in my experience there had never been such happiness. And I would never love anyone else as I would learn to love him.

With his love, Bill would give me what then became my life—his daily, improbable being, his friendship, his understanding, his observations, his ideas, his response to writing, his humor, his support, his warm comfort. Together we would seek out the rocking chair, the china, the towels, the scores of material things for our home. Together, we would face and fumble with all the intangibles in the pleasure of being alive. Over four decades, we stayed together as a couple. We stayed together as we found and raised a child. We shared the child. We shared our work. We shared our home. We shared our thoughts. I never fully stopped being a writer, but he enabled me to become also, in effect if not in name, a wife to him and then, with a child, a mother. I don't think I missed anything. And miraculously, he told me, I was able to give him a measure of "belief" in his own "reality," as well as freedom and some release from his "cell." I would go on long drives on a highway with him, when time would be suspended, and he would not seem to care about the exact distance from an exit. I would go with him to see a show—in particular, *Pacific Overtures*—and emerge, still warmly lost in the show, into a below-zero night, historically one of the coldest of that year (1976), without a flinch. Whatever flowed between us and gave us warmth made us both feel fully alive.

We were drawn to each other from the first by all the elusive forces that people have been trying to pin down from the beginning of time. When, by the early 1950s, we were committed to each other—never to change—we tried once or twice to pin them down for ourselves, but as both of us were constitutionally resistant to theorizing, we gave up, merging with each other instead in our physical joy and pleasure, and in laughter.

Our communication over our joint work may have been one point of departure for what happened. But it was only

We walked, arm in arm, all over the city. One afternoon Bill was wearing his sporty cap when a street photographer snapped our picture. It was about four o'clock; Bill always called it his "hour of hope."

one. When Bill took it further, his undisguised emotional expression of what he found in me was initially terrifying. I felt: Not *me*, for God's sake! I want to keep my mind on my *writing*! I was probably as far as it's possible to be from embodying the femme fatale. And with Bill Shawn's wife and children belying "there but not there"—even though to him this contradiction was a statement of fact, and he made it seem so to me—there were complications stemming from the fact. It would not be an acceptable fact to my family or to a court of law or to the pope. The complications were too much for me to handle. I tried to run away from it, and I took off for California. I remained there, away from him, for about a year and a half. But that simply didn't work. The odds may have been against our being together, but my attempt at *not* being together turned out to be doomed.

As was well known, Bill Shawn spent years in working harmony with scores and scores of renowned writers, artists, editors, publishers, agents, and colleagues. Many people looked to him almost worshipfully to help them realize and express their talent. The greatest beneficiaries of Bill's attention were the writers. For at least fifty years, he worked closely with some of the most sensitive, perceptive, talented, and sophisticated writers anywhere in the world. He lunched with them and sat with them for hours going over their manuscripts. He was their friend; he tried to be what he called "a giver of compassion and understanding." They accepted the compassion and understanding—and they gloried in his creative and material help. They knew him in a certain way. "I write for *you*," his authors would say to him. They all said the same words: "I write for *you*." He would look embarrassed when they said it to him. If someone he didn't think was a wonderful writer said it to him, he would look doubly embarrassed. All writers gratefully took what he gave them. He didn't reveal to them what this effort cost him. "They do not question my peculiarities" is how he put it.

Some of the writers who did not question his "peculiarities" loved Bill for his total dedication to their writing. He tried to keep his dedication unspoiled by his sharp awareness—in the case of a few—of intolerable egotism, of ruthless opportunism, of special pleading, of greed, of descent into mediocrity. "They are unfortunate," he would say thoughtfully. Although he kept his sharpness and his skepticism under total control, he usually sensed the truth of everybody around him.

By his own choice, and whatever the toll to himself, including life itself, he tuned in to the deepest wishes of others and tried to give them what *they* wanted. "Unpleasant" was his strongest word for what he felt about the character of the few who repelled him. He was usually able to reject writing that was unacceptable for one reason or another, but once in a while, in order to protect the feelings of a writer, he would buy a piece, pay the writer, and hold the work in the "bank" for years. He bought and published work of a couple of writers he felt personally sorry for. His rationalization in these instances was always one that essentially satisfied him. It was on a plane that I did not fully grasp until I had lived with him for many years. It went something like this: "Every human being is as valuable as every other human being, and it is important to me not to hurt this person." To Bill Shawn, every life was sacred. I would occasionally question him about the subject, about what seemed to be the issue of "honesty." He was never perturbed. He would always preface his answer by saying "It's very complicated, but in the deepest way..."

Although Bill would devote days and nights to helping his writers and artists with personal problems of every imaginable kind, he never encouraged people to get into his own personal life. His oldest friends somehow knew he had marked a line beyond which he did not wish them to step. He was on a first-name basis with a few longtime friends in his office, but he had difficulty in addressing most people by their first names. Their addressing him as "Mr. Shawn" was fine with him. His manner was the same with everybody—genuinely democratic and respectful. His courtesy to all visitors—escorting them out of his office and to the elevator—became legendary. He would see anybody, including *all* job seekers, who wrote asking for an appointment. Away from the office, he usually kept to the same mode. To everybody on his staff he was courteous, considerate, and tolerant. He never raised his voice. He almost never permitted himself to reveal rage. He kept his distance from other people by keeping the concentration on them. All of his writers experienced his intense and immediately sympathetic attention to them. Everyone noticed his unmistakable intelligence, and everyone soaked up his unmistakable affection.

When Bill and I became a couple, his way of distancing himself from other people turned out to be a useful framework for us. People left us alone. From the beginning to the end of our years together, we usually had no need to be with anyone else. Neither he nor I needed to talk to other people about our life together. People in the office were our friends, some closer than others, but mostly Bill and I wanted to be alone with each other. We never tired of this self-imposed isolation; we liked it that way. Occasionally, we might have dinner at a restaurant with another couple, or go with others to the theatre or to listen to jazz. But neither of us seemed to need a "social life." In fact, we couldn't understand why other couples needed a regular pattern of "doing things" in groups. Bill and I seemed perpetually interested only in being with each other.

After a while, our colleagues got to know about us. They saw us arrive at the office together. They saw us leave together. They saw us together at the theatre, at concerts, on the city's streets, in the park. They saw us going into our house and coming out of our house. If they gossiped about us, we didn't hear it. Most people seemed to honor our privacy.

About himself, Bill spoke to me unhistrionically and quietly, with detachment, and without self-indulgence. "Why am I more ghost than man?" he would ask softly. Over the years, he asked me time and again, "Do you know who I am?" He spoke in his usual gentle tone. At the end of one of our leisurely, time-free Saturday afternoons together, he might say, "Please do not let me forget my own life." And occasionally he might add, "It's someone else's life that I have lived."

He loved gaiety and innocence and joy and sexy women, preferably Europeans, and he longed for the earthiest and wildest kinds of sexual adventures. He was, as I said, romantic. His favorite words were "magical" and "enchanting." He was drawn to all forms of humor, especially writing that made him laugh, and he contributed his astonishing talents to making the work of others more telling in every way, preferably funnier. While he admired erudition, he reveled in comedy, and writing and comic art that made him laugh. He reveled in S. J. Perelman, and he was sent soaring by J. D. Salinger and Ian Frazier and Joe Mitchell and Ed Koren and Roz Chast and William Steig. Drawings by Saul Steinberg or Sempé rendered him almost mute with awe. Eagerly, he sought out old-time vaudeville comics, such as Willie Howard and Smith and Dale. He was at one with Groucho Marx as well as with Buster Keaton. He tried always to watch the English comic Benny Hill on television. He went for classic Jewish joke-telling. Myron Cohen, he would say, had the best dialect of the lot. When we watched Myron Cohen appearing on the Johnny Carson show, Bill's entire body would pulse with delight, especially when Cohen would affect his special heavy-lidded, phony "elegance" in the ethnic accent. In the 1960s, we went repeatedly to see the *Beyond the Fringe* foursome on Broadway. Bill could be restored by Richard Pryor. I went with him to see *Spinal Tap* several times. He waited eagerly for theatrical or cinematic glimpses of Walter Matthau and Zero Mostel and Robin Williams in any role. He

I was completely occupied with thoughts about myself. I was going to do the work I loved. I didn't want anything else. I was ecstatic.

He would say he could not go outside in a heavy storm, rain or snow, or in a deep freeze. We went ice-skating at Grossinger's. He was able, surprisingly, to stretch his limits.

While confiding to me desperate thoughts about himself, he still would tell me how lucky we were to be in whatever day or whatever hour or whatever instant we were in together.

was both knocked out by and inspired by the subtle, inimitable humor of Ralph Richardson and Alec Guinness. He was drawn to show business in general—to all musical comedy, from Busby Berkeley movies to Comden and Green concoctions to anything touched by composers from Cole Porter to Stephen Sondheim. We went half a dozen times to see Laurence Olivier on the stage in *The Entertainer*, and as many times again to see it with Olivier on the screen.

Bill Shawn's deepest satisfactions, however, were listening to and playing jazz. He responded with every muscle in his body to jazz. He knew and loved classical music, but the music closest to his heart was the popular music that lent itself to jazz improvisation. He had his own way, privately and seriously, of admiring intellectuality. He rejoiced in beautiful art, beautiful writing, and beautiful thinking. He liked Kierkegaard and Proust and Musil, but he worshiped Duke Ellington.

All his life, even as a child, Bill Shawn felt and feared his own death. It was always with him. When he was still in his forties or fifties, he would awaken in surprise that he was still alive. "I'm still here," he would say in the morning, imparting the observation seriously and undramatically. In his later years, he occasionally philosophized about why we want to go on living, despite suffering, despite pain, despite disappointment. By then he was revealing in the way he looked, the way he walked, the way he laughed, that he was doing just that, wanting to live, *living*. I didn't have to talk about that one with him. It was because of everything he had opened me up to in life that I was able in some measure to make my return in kind.

Although he feared dying, he had often felt suicidal, he told me. Many times when we were reunited, after a night apart, the first thing that he mentioned to me was the "punishment" he had to endure because of the pain he had inflicted on Cecille. He would say that suicide was in his mind. But he fought against it. "I'm trying to hack my way out of this despair," he would say.

Overwhelming all else was Bill's feeling that he did not exist. "Who has declared me null and void?" he would ask me politely. He was a clear and logical thinker. If he did not exist, there was nothing to reveal to people. For years, he kept his agonies and his occasional hopes secret.

This was the man I loved.

CHAPTER 2

FINDING THE NEW YORKER

William Shawn hired me as a reporter for *The New Yorker* in February 1945, a few months before the end of World War II in Europe. I had one priority: reporting and writing. All of my energy was channeled into that work. For the time being, it was everything I wanted. I did not long for marriage. I did not long for anyone to share my life with. I had no interest in assuming responsibility for anyone's life but my own.

Bill would become the editor-in-chief in 1952, after the death of Harold Ross, the founder and first editor of the magazine. When I first met Bill, he was thirty-seven years old and had been the managing editor for six years. By then he had been given carte blanche by Harold Ross to develop what was becoming the magazine's great tradition of literary journalism—original ways of writing nonfiction stories, including spectacular and innovative reporting about the war.

I was ostensibly "interviewed" by Bill for the job in his small, spare office, on the nineteenth floor at 25 West Forty-third Street. He sat at a wooden table holding neatly stacked long galley proofs and a cup filled with freshly sharpened black, eraser-topped pencils. I took a scruffy, upholstered armchair alongside. I had been working for a few years for an upstart tabloid newspaper, *PM,* where cigarette-smoking editors in shirtsleeves were loudly confident in manner and fairly unkempt. In contrast, Bill looked quiet and uncertain. He wore a white shirt, a dark-blue necktie, and a gray tweed suit, and he kept his jacket on, buttoned. He was hesitant, self-conscious, almost apologetic, and seemed not to know what questions to ask me. He looked boyish. I immediately noticed the unmistakable honesty in his face. The fullness of his mouth, the blueness of his eyes registered. I was aware of an unplaceable familiar feeling about him. He stared at me for a long time in that first meeting, almost as though his speech were frozen. I mentioned the marvelous writing of E. B. White and Joseph Mitchell and A. J. Liebling, and he seemed pleased and responded with the word "Yes," which was somehow punctuated with a restrained sob. Bill offered me a job at seventy-five dollars a week, twice my salary at *PM.* I said nothing. I nodded. I left his office in a daze. I was completely occupied with thoughts about myself. I was going to do the work I loved. I didn't want anything else. I didn't want to be anywhere else. I was ecstatic.

Bill Shawn had the exceptional capacity it took to tune in to Harold Ross in every way and to serve him so imaginatively as to give him what he wanted and needed before he knew he wanted and needed it. But Bill's talents went far beyond all that. Bill was also a poet and a writer. To others, he disparaged his own gift for writing, but he was always ready to give bits and pieces of it—whatever his artists or writers needed—to all of us. But more than anything else in his makeup, quietly, without thinking about it or making it necessary for anybody else to think about it, he was always able to establish a powerfully creative connection with each of the hundreds of writers and artists he worked with. He was able to feel what each one was capable of creating, and he could

I immediately noticed the unmistakable honesty in his face. The fullness of his mouth, the blueness of his eyes, registered. I was aware of an unplaceable familiarity about him.

My enjoyment of the "work" was endless. I would be laughing in anticipation of what I would write.

guide each one to express and realize that creation. It was almost as though his own creativity encompassed everyone else's. He possessed the single most important quality that creative people hunger for: he was able to connect with their talent. It seemed that wherever anyone wanted to go in his work, Bill Shawn had already been there, or was eager to be there, so he could show the writer or the artist the way to go.

I didn't have a clue, at the beginning, about the deep turmoil going on within him. As he worked with the people who looked to him for what they needed to realize their talent, he would wonder about his own life and what he called his "ghostly aspect," his "transparency" and the "silence" of his footsteps. I learned later how he would grieve over his "secret self."

"I can grieve over it, but I cannot change it," he would eventually say to me.

As the editor I was working for, Bill was direct, clear, professional, and, from the very beginning, sympathetic. I found no hint of any "secret self" about him. He was utterly in tune with me, and I concentrated happily on the work. Naturally, like my colleagues, I emitted all the usual signs of needing the encouragement, the appreciation, and the inspiration that led to original, solid reporting and writing, especially writing that would make him laugh. From the start, I found that I *could* make him laugh. His face, as open and receptive as a child's, would break up with an expression that seemed to start with joy but wound up as that sob. I noticed it but didn't question it. I also began to notice that his unusual facial expresssions stayed with me, flashing in my head at odd moments. They were unexpected, moving, unsettling.

Before coming to *The New Yorker,* I had started, of all things, the *Chinese Student Magazine,* at the request of a young man named Raymond Yo. My name had been given to him by one of my former teachers. I knew nothing about China, but I admired Raymond Yo's impeccable manners and impeccable suits, so I set about creating a magazine. For our first issue, I got Milton Caniff, creator of my favorite comic strip, *Terry and the Pirates,* to do a drawing of his Terry character for the cover (for free); inside, the magazine ran material that reported, more or less, on Chinese students in the United States.

Then I went to work at *PM,* which had been started by Ralph Ingersoll, an alumnus of *The New Yorker* and of *Life* magazine. I worked in *PM*'s morgue-library and learned a lot about newspaper reporting by reading hundreds of the stories I was filing from dozens of major newspapers and magazines. Then I switched over to *PM*'s Sunday magazine section, for which I wrote stories for a kind of imitation of "Talk of the Town" that was called "Local Items." I was having a lot of fun running around with a photographer named Skippy Adelman in tow, catching, for example, Clare Boothe Luce at a dinner party and appropriating her tablecloth doodles (self-portraits), which were published along with my story. I followed the visiting General Charles de Gaulle with Mayor La Guardia to the top of the Empire State Building, squirmed to a position directly behind them, and reported the general's striking question "*Où est la Coney Island?*" (The quote was used as a caption for a photograph of me, standing behind the general and taking notes, which was published in a magazine.) I wrote a story about William Steig, the great comic artist, then doing beautiful, innovative artwork in *The New Yorker* and in his books *About People, All Embarrassed,* and *Small Fry.* That was over fifty years ago, and I've been a fan of his, and we've been friends, ever since.

My "Local Items" editor was an attractive, elegant, self-deprecating young woman, Peggy Wright, newly married to the writer Jerome Weidman. (They are the parents of the playwright John Weidman.) One day Peggy told me she was going over to *The New Yorker* office during her lunch hour to meet with William Shawn, who wanted her to work for him as an assistant. When Peggy came back to the *PM* office, she told me that Shawn was just the kind of man she would like to work for. But she had decided against moving to *The New Yorker* because she was going to quit working altogether in order to devote herself full-time to her marriage. She urged me to go to see Shawn, in case I wanted to work for him. Before I went, I read, in a few issues of *The New Yorker:* a "Reporter at Large" by A. J. Liebling that started out, "Three days after the first Allied landing in France, I was in the wardroom of an LCIL (Landing Craft Infantry Large) off the Normandy coast..."; a Profile of Duke Ellington entitled "The Hot Bach," by Richard O. Boyer; a humor piece, "Take Two Parts Sand, One Part Girl and Stir," by S. J. Perelman; a "Reporter at Large" by Joseph Mitchell about Hugh G. Flood, aged ninety-four, "inviting me to come down to his hotel in the Fulton Fish Market district and help him eat a bushel of black clams..." (fiction in the form of fact, but that was a secret for a long, long time); Charles Addams with his Family; Helen Hokinson with her Ladies; and Saul Steinberg, drawing from war-coping Italy. It would be an understatement to say I liked the magazine. I was transported by it. I knew immediately that this magazine was where I wanted to be.

Before I arrived at *The New Yorker,* three other women had been hired to fill in for the men fighting in, and/or reporting from, the armed services. Many of the great reporters were still away. David Lardner (one of several Lardners, including Ring, John, Susan, Rex, and James, to come to the magazine) had recently been killed when his jeep ran into a land mine in Germany. It was in an atmosphere of sadness over the first young casualty among the writers, together with awe of the journalistic giants, that the first female general reporters, all in their early twenties and all hired by Bill, walked in the magazine's dark, seedy, terrifying, and hallowed halls. We had been notified, one way or another, of Harold Ross's extreme reluctance to have us there. He took a dim view of working with women, who were—he was quoted to us as saying crossly—"trouble." I was prepared to take resistance to women reporters in stride. Ever since I was thirteen years old, I had read and re-read and re-read again the book *City Editor* by Stanley Walker, the legendary city editor of the *New York Herald Tribune,* a great newspaper. Walker had written in his book that he did not like to have women working in his city room because they cry. I determined that I would be different from any of the newspaperwomen Stanley Walker might have known; no matter what happened, I would never, never cry. (Walker himself did a brief stint as an editor under Ross, but after about a year he went back to the *Herald Tribune.* A few years after I started working for Harold Ross and William Shawn, I happened to visit the *Herald Tribune*'s city room and was introduced to Stanley Walker, who turned out to be charming and courteous, with an old-fashioned and warmly respectful manner toward women.)

Like the other women hired by *The New Yorker,* I worked as a reporter mainly for "The Talk of the Town." Bill, looking embarrassed, told me: "You may not like the work. We want you to write *facts.*" I assured him that I had a friendly attachment to facts. I was preceded by Andy Logan, the first woman to be hired—the day after she graduated from Swarthmore in 1942—as a general staff reporter. Roseanne Smith, the late Scottie (Frances Scott Fitzgerald) Lanahan, and I followed three years later. My three colleagues among the pioneer women at the magazine were all good reporters. Andy Logan was strong, reliable, admirably informed, energetic, skeptical, courageous, and a skillful writer (as she still is). While she was eight months pregnant, she climbed up a rope ladder in order to get aboard a vessel at the Brooklyn Navy Yard. Roseanne Smith seemed to me to be a model for *The Front Page*'s Hildy Johnson, as played by Rosalind Russell, with Cary Grant, in *His Girl Friday*—an impression that was confirmed when I was unable to get past police lines to report on the crowds at the

We had been notified, one way or another, of Harold Ross's extreme reluctance to have us there. He took a dim view of working with women.

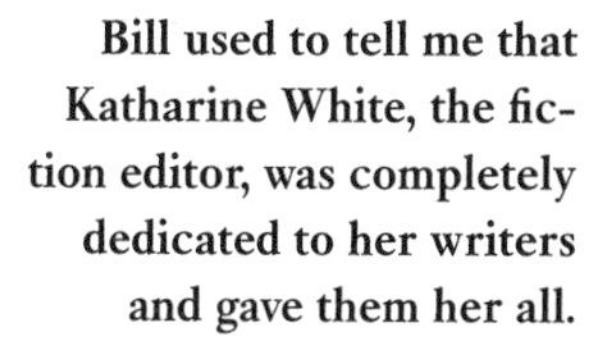

Bill used to tell me that Katharine White, the fiction editor, was completely dedicated to her writers and gave them her all.

The rewrite man—most of the time, he turned out to be Brendan Gill—ran our "notes" through the typewriter and made a few changes so that the voice would be perceived as male.

A. J. Liebling used to walk around the corridors with a quizzical expression on his face. It would grow more quizzical whenever he commented on the way I wrote, asking me why I didn't give my opinions in my pieces.

Joe Mitchell, author of the remarkable "McSorley's Wonderful Saloon," and Joe Liebling. As far as I was concerned, Joe and Joe could do no wrong. I was proud of a photograph I took of them together outside our office building.

Philip Hamburger would pop into my office and do funny imitations of people in the news. Bill would say that Hamburger should have been a comic actor. I was in a constant state of happiness over these wonderful, inspirational people who had become my fellow writers.

Empire State Building the year the infamous plane crashed into it. "I did not have a police press pass," I explained lamely to Bill, who responded, "Roseanne *Smith* got through, and Roseanne *Smith* didn't have a police press pass." Scottie Lanahan, in addition to being very pretty and very smart, was high-spirited and funny. She was a good egg and fun to hang out with. Also, she was a good writer; she worked hard and bravely concealed the pain of growing up as the daughter of Scott and Zelda, as well as her loneliness when she lived with her father's literary agent, Harold Ober, and his wife, who did their best to take care of her. Scottie had recently been married to Jack Lanahan, a young lawyer, who had then been drafted into the Army, and so she was still living with the Obers.

All of us were reporters, yes, but we were not going to be allowed to write what were called "Talk of the Town originals." We were to write "notes." The notes would be given to a rewrite man so that he could give the stories a "masculine point of view." This was Harold Ross's idea. The rewrite man—most of the time he turned out to be Brendan Gill—ran our "notes" through the typewriter and made a few changes so that the voice would be perceived as male.

One of my first Talk stories was about Harry Truman as a haberdasher. By telephone, I located and interviewed Edward Jacobson in Kansas City—formerly of Truman & Jacobson, Shirts, Collars, Hosiery, Gloves, Belts and Hats. ("Harry was a great salesman. He didn't push a shirt or tie at you; he made you feel you needed to buy it.") Brendan Gill began the rewrite of my effort this way: "One of our younger assistants was going through Kansas City and among the people *he* [my italics] spoke to was Edward Jacobson..." Scottie Lanahan and I had some good giggles about the way Gill changed our gender, but we had endless admiration for Gill's facile, exemplary, elegant, instructive prose. All of us were good, non-troublemaking women. It never occurred to me, at least, to

The extraordinary caricaturist Abe Birnbaum, one of the host of writers and artists who were now my colleagues, walked into my office one day and drew this.

combat the methodology of the "masculine point of view." At any rate, it disintegrated under Bill, gradually but completely.

I was still in love with reporting, all right, but now I was pinning my love on a magazine. Inside the glossy covers every week, I found the combined creation not only of Harold Ross and William Shawn but of a host of writers and artists who were my idols. Every morning, on my way to 25 West Forty-third Street, I couldn't contain my excitement over my good fortune to have become part of that place. The closer I came to the office, the louder and faster my heartbeat grew. (Finally, I knew what *that* cliché meant.) In the elevator, going up, I was afraid that other people could hear the din inside my body. The wonderful reporters and writers I met in the dimly-lighted corridors were now my *colleagues.* When I saw Bill Shawn, I enjoyed his enthusiastic interest in me as one of his reporters, and I enjoyed looking at his face, but I didn't seek anything other than his praise and his response to what I was writing. If, from time to time, I noted anything else, I put it aside. I wasn't going to let anything disturb my concentration on this work of mine. I didn't know it, but this would change. Bill's spirit, all-encompassing as it became in the pages of *The New Yorker,* extended far beyond the magazine, and I would not be able to turn away from it.

CHAPTER 3

THREADS OF CONNECTION

Eventually, I discovered that there were congruencies between Bill's beginnings and mine. Neither Bill nor I was a native New Yorker. He was born in Chicago. I was born in Syracuse, New York. Bill was the youngest of five children, the eldest of whom, Harold, was sixteen, and his sister, Melba, was fourteen when Bill was born. Bill had two other older brothers—Nelson and Michael. To all of them, as long as they lived, Bill was "Billy," the one to be shielded in every way from hurt, from evil, from ugliness, from the facts and instances of illness and death. His brothers were musical, and they introduced Bill to playing jazz. Harold played the violin; Nelson wrote songs; Michael wrote advertising jingles.

Both of our fathers were protective of women. We were both very close to our mothers, and we learned that they were similar. Both had Eastern European roots. Both were shy, gentle, romantic, warm, humble, and unsophisticated. They were non-intellectual and centered on the happiness of their children. Bill told me that his mother, who came with her family from Canada and who died in Chicago at the age of eighty-nine, had little interest in the world outside of her children. My mother had a good deal of curiosity and some wistful longings to know about everything in the worlds beyond her own. She wrote sentimental poetry about love and hid her poems in the far corners of drawers. After her death—of a heart attack at the age of forty-nine—I discovered her handwritten poems.

Both Bill's family and mine were Jewish on both sides, and neither of us had a formally religious upbringing. I had never entered a synagogue or understood what went on inside one until I was fifteen, when a friend took me to an Orthodox service. My father had great humor. His humor was original. His thinking was independent. He disliked the nouveaux riches and social climbers. He despised superficiality and snobbery and cloddishness. He was put off by cold or literal-minded people; he was drawn to warmth and intelligence and laughter. He had a garage, and he loved cars and working on cars. He enjoyed working with his hands, and using his hands to make cars look beautiful. He would spend five times longer than was called for in order to satisfy himself in his work. He rarely thought about money in relation to his work; he told his customers to pay him whatever and whenever they chose. He did not know how to explain his economic philosophy to my mother, who had to buy the groceries.

My father's ideas about the male-female equation were standard Victorian, but touching. And somehow, conservative and limited as his ideas sounded, his bottom-line feelings about the sexes nevertheless stayed with me. In his view, women were frailer then men; they needed men for strength, for support, for inspiration. He had contempt for a man who took money from a woman. He disliked pretentious intellectuals and self-centered dilettantes, he used to say, because they sat around in cafeterias talking and talking and never doing any honest work. And *they,* he said, took money from women. He was a reader, in Russian, of the great Russian writers. He never ran with any pack. Both Bill's father and mine were hot-tempered, stubborn, rebellious, and highly intelligent. Bill's father, energetic and entrepreneurial, was apolitical, but, Bill told me, he might have voted Republican. My father was a two-time political escapee from Siberian prisons. He was one of the first Socialists in Republican-dominated Syracuse. The "ism" I identified with in my youth was socialism, not Judaism.

My father moved our family to the most conservative suburb of the city and promptly enraged all our neighbors by raising and harboring hundreds of pigeons in the roof space of our garage. The neighbors' hostility was only partially diffused when my brother invited his friends to use his basketball hoop in the backyard. The neighbors regarded my father's garden with disdain—his sunflowers (instead of delicate pansies), as well as his prosaic radishes and cucumbers and tomatoes, which we picked on summer nights for our dinner. Even our emotionally demonstrative female dog came in for derision because she was a small curly-haired mongrel who daily followed my brother and sister and me to school and generously made herself available to any male dogs who showed interest in her. She gave birth to several litters of puppies, which were entrusted to our care. I guarded those puppies with my life. Our next-door neighbors, the Beckwiths, very proper and sedate, who optimistically hoped to reform us, brought Christian Science literature to my mother to try to show her the way.

Both Bill and I felt Jewish, especially when it came to humor, but we didn't think in terms of Jewishness for our "identity." Both of us seemed to be comfortable with the heritage without any formality over it. About the only times I questioned Bill's Jewishness were in connection with (1) his whole-hearted preference for bread that was white and limp and (2) his compulsion to be utterly forgiving and kind to people who were rude or cruel or opportunistic or destructive or insulting toward him. He was never vindictive, and he would never, never hit back. At those times, I would wonder to myself: Why is this man trying to be more Christian than a Christian?

My father died in 1950—of lung cancer brought on by constant inhalation of lead paint fumes—at the age of sixty. Bill heard of his death, and although they had never met, Bill told me, looking upset, that he wished he had been able to be of some help to me during my father's illness. Bill had been working very closely with me at the time on some long pieces that eventually got considerable attention—about Hollywood during the Communist witch-hunt, about a bullfighter from Brooklyn, about the Miss America beauty contest, and about Ernest Hemingway. Although my father took pride in my early writing for *The New Yorker,* when he somehow or other picked up word of my growing friendship with Bill Shawn he was dismayed enough to express anger and disapproval to my brother. My father never said a word to me about it. He kept his worries to himself.

Bill's father, Benjamin Chon (Bill changed the spelling of his name because he thought it sounded misleadingly Chinese), stubbornly refused to move his silver, diamonds, and cutlery business, the Jackknife Shop, out of the Chicago meat-packing area even though he was almost the last one there who had nothing to do with meat. Bill told me his father, who was known in the neighborhood as Jackknife Ben, was widely respected and admired for his diligence and honesty. He died in 1952 at the age of eighty-nine. Bill's father was strict. "I was afraid of him," Bill told me. "Unlike my brothers and sister, who might do things to make my father angry, I just tried not to be noticed by him. My mother, however, was easygoing and indulgent."

Ever since childhood I have been an observer. The youngest of three children, I was a constant observer of my older brother, Simeon, and my sister, Helen. They had many friends of their age. I had none. The role of outsider is a lonely one, especially for a child, but I can't remember being particularly unhappy. On Saturday afternoons, when other children, including my two siblings, always seemed to have someone to go to the movies with, I went alone. My father would drive me to the theatre, press an enormous silver half-dollar into my hand, and wish me a happy movie. Sitting by myself, waiting for the movie to start, holding my Clark Bar and Cracker Jack box, I would be quietly satisfied to observe the restless antics of other children around me. When I started baby-sitting the four-year-old boy from across the street whose father drank, whose parents fought, and who regularly had a gorgeous Christmas tree, I, too, had somebody to go to the movies with.

At *The New Yorker,* logically and cheerfully, I relished the role of reporter-writer. I rejoiced in the challenge of creating, in my own small way, a surprise for the creative force behind the magazine. I don't know what elicits the work of my fellow writers; for me it has always been—and is still—the spirit of the single person in charge of making the publication a living entity. An appreciative response to my offerings was all I wanted.

When I was working, I needed no diversions. I engaged in outside activities out of curiosity or dutifulness or a need to please someone else. Once, without any musical talent whatsoever, I took clarinet lessons—with Reginald Kell, a Yorkshireman who played classical clarinet duets with Benny Goodman—for no reason that makes any sense, and after a while, I gave the clarinet away to a schoolchild I was writing about. I played tennis ferociously in order to have something to hit. My true interest lay in other people; it never occurred to me to be of interest to myself. Perhaps that is why I was never drawn to psychoanalysis. I was bored by most of what I knew of it, and I felt very sorry for friends who were passively led—some for years, or even a lifetime—by their doctors' arbitrary interpretations of Freudian precepts. I enjoyed my empathies. I hardly ever looked at myself in a mirror.

I was aware of the fact that I was not unappealing. I had been my parents' favorite and my older sister's protégée, and I don't think I had much in the way of adolescent objections to myself. As a child, I had a round face and extremely curly hair, and I kept those features, more or less, all the way up the line. It was a useful look that seemed to go with being a listener, not a talker. I was always interested in the person I was with, and I discovered that everybody liked having a listener. I accepted friendship, but I rarely pursued it. I enjoyed men and maleness, and I had boyfriends, but I ducked involvement with anyone who seemed to want more than uncomplicated pleasure and a casual routine of parties and movies and plays and dinner dates. I had writing to do for myself, and I wanted to be left alone to do it. I was not prepared for any cataclysmic entanglement of my life with that of anyone else.

During Bill's entire lifetime, starting with what he called the "crazed blandness" of his childhood, he had the overriding feeling that he must never feel trapped, never be closed in. He told me that when his mother took him, at the age of six, to his first day of school, she asked his teacher, a Miss Mok, to give him a pass to leave school whenever he needed to go home. "Miss Mok was very sympathetic and understanding and told my mother it would never become an issue," Bill said. I was moved by Bill's respectful and deferential mention of "Miss Mok," as though he were still six and Miss Mok were just around the corner. As he grew older, his mother discovered that he had other fears—of blood, of violence, of the dark, of heights—and she accepted those, also. "My fears penned me in," Bill told me.

In elementary school, for the first six years, Bill was a poor student and was completely bewildered by all his subjects, especially arithmetic. By seventh grade he was enrolled in the Harvard School for Boys on the South Side (the school only recently dropped "for Boys"), and immediately he started earning high grades, the highest in his class in English. He helped his classmates with their schoolwork. When he was fourteen, he wrote an entire novel for an older friend. Then he embarked on writing another novel, for himself, but he gave it up near the end. "I do not wish to go on with it," he told his mother. "It is not what I wish to write."

About that time, a terrible thrill-murder of a neighborhood boy was committed by two young men, also from that neighborhood. They were Nathan Leopold and Richard Loeb. Their victim, Bobby Franks, was a few years younger than Bill, who was then sixteen and small for his age. Leopold and Loeb had stopped in at Bill's house a short time before the murder. Bill told me about it. "I barely knew them when, for no apparent reason, they came to our kitchen and kept staring at me," he said. "They were, I imagine, looking me over as a candidate for what they were going to do." That experience would haunt him. He could feel the death of the murdered boy.

Bill told me he was what was known as a "good boy." He was neat and clean and quiet. His family lived in a three-story gray-stone house on Vincennes Avenue on the South Side of Chicago. Bill used to describe the house as "ugly," but then he would add, "It was ugly and enchanting, and I loved it more than any other house I've lived in since."

At the age of twelve, Bill came down with scarlet fever, and his nurse, quarantined with him in his room, decided he needed, in addition to nursing, some sexual education. "To my astonishment, she provided both, but I don't think it did me any harm," Bill told me.

Much as his siblings tried to protect him, Bill knew tragedy. His brother Nelson died of a heart attack at the age of forty-seven. Nelson had written the popular song "Jim," and Bill often played it for me movingly, combining it, at my request, with Jerome Kern's "Bill." Much later, Bill would experience

Bill was known to friends and family as a "good boy." He was neat and quiet. He helped his classmates with their schoolwork. When he was fourteen, he wrote an entire novel for an older friend.

I guarded those puppies with my life.

an overwhelming tragedy with his daughter, Mary. He had noticed early, before anyone else saw it, he told me, that Mary was not developing normally, and in time it was confirmed that she had been born brain-damaged. It became necessary eventually to send her away from home, to a special school out of town. After that, Bill saw Mary only when she was brought home for visits. He used to tell me how musical she was, how she played the piano. He would report that she was putting on some weight, or that she had had her hair cut short. She had no real sense of time, he said, so on each visit she greeted everybody as though no time had passed since the last one. Bill would report all this in a deliberately controlled, reasonable way, trying to conceal the anguish in his face.

Bill's "bland" childhood included a lot of roller-skating and baseball-playing in neighborhood lots with his closest friend, his first cousin, Marshall Berman, and with other friends. "I knew all the batting averages of the Chicago White Sox," Bill told me proudly. For years he longed to have a pony, complete with pony cart. He would imagine driving in his pony cart on excursions to other neighborhoods, to go on errands. He even selected the color of his cart—pastel blue. He never realized his dream, but he never let go of it. (Years later, we wrote a children's story together about a little boy getting a pony with a pastel-blue cart.) For vacations, he went to the Catskills with his parents. One summer in the mountains, during his early teens, Bill had an adolescent liaison with Molly Berg, who became the writer of the tremendously popular radio series called *The Goldbergs.*

He became addicted early to going to the movies and to vaudeville shows, usually at Chicago's Palace Theatre. His steady companion was his maternal grandmother. She was bent over from osteoporosis, and she walked very slowly. Every Saturday afternoon, from the time he was about ten, they walked to the theatre together, holding hands; he would be impatient—inconsiderate, as children often are with the elderly—and would urge her to walk faster. He remembered that impatience with guilt and pain for the rest of his life. He always referred to her as "my little grandmother." Their faces were similar, he told me, no matter the difference in their age—round faces, high cheekbones, large, warm, sensual mouths. He had picked up from her, he once told me, his habit of holding his teacup backwards, embracing it with the handle side turned in, his hand around the middle.

The pure light-blue color of Bill's eyes became one of the mystical threads of our connection. When I was five years old, living in Syracuse, my mother gave birth to a baby boy, Teddy, who was born brain-damaged. He lived for about a year and a half. He could not cry, could not speak, could not sit, could not walk. Day after day, his face would be contorted, and as I watched him, he seemed to be trying to utter sounds, but they came out as choked moans. I observed my mother's excruciating sadness and exhaustion day after day, as she took care of the baby, feeding him and cleaning him. I watched the parade of strange, grim-faced doctors who came to examine him. On the midwinter day of Teddy's death, there was a big snowstorm, and that evening, for the first time in my life, I heard my father sobbing loudly, outside, where he had gone to grieve, shoveling snow.

Teddy was a beautiful baby, with soft, curly blond hair and pure light-blue eyes. Exactly like Bill's. Exactly like my father's eyes, for that matter. I used to stand daily at Teddy's crib, looking into his eyes, trying to *will* him to cry, *will* him to speak, to walk, to make noise, to be a *baby.* I would say his name, "Teddy," over and over again. One day, standing at the crib, I made eye contact with Teddy, and I got him (or thought I got him) to echo "Teddy." I felt that this response was a triumph. The purity and beauty of that baby's face, the plea that I saw in his pure blue eyes, stayed in my consciousness all my life. There is no mystery in my lifelong search for that pleading look.

After Teddy died, my two older siblings became inordinately protective of me. (My brother, Simeon, still is.) When we got our dog, who would have our puppies, we named her Teddy. My sister, Helen, was supersensitive, perceptive, and original, and I believed she knew everything. If I was taken in, deceived, or misled by somebody, she would set me straight. She had a kind of telepathic line to the truth about everyone and everything. I never found her to be proven wrong. When she was ten, she told me that someday she was going to be a "traveling correspondent." She told me she would go all over the world, writing stories. So I appropriated her idea, and I never imagined there would be anything else for me to do as work.

Helen could not stand to see anyone in pain. Only four years older than I was, she used to take the baby Teddy into bed with her every night to try to comfort him. She was my mentor in every way. She had infallible instincts for what was good and for what looked good. She taught me what "taste" meant in clothes. We both had very curly hair. Mine was thicker than hers, and unmanageable. One day, when I was about eleven, she cut off most of it and declared that I must wear it short. I haven't changed it since.

In my adolescence, I started resisting Helen's insights, her perceptions, her critical evaluations of this one or that one. She immediately recognized fraudulence, cruelty, hostility, the entire roster of negatives to be feared and avoided. She might be right on the button, but it often took me years to appreciate the accuracy of her perceptions. In her late teens and twenties she was a classically beautiful girl, a fact that was acknowledged with unanimity and enthusiasm in our family. She had the kind of attractiveness and wistful, feminine appeal—especially to men—that invariably made her noticed as soon as she entered a room.

I took her along one day to meet Ernest Hemingway and his wife, Mary, with whom I had become chummy. Marlene

Dietrich, who was a grandmother by then and on the downward spiral of her career, happened to drop in while we were having a drink. After Helen and I left, we talked about the Hemingways and about Marlene Dietrich. Starry-eyed, I said I thought the actress was glamorous.

"Yes, but I could feel her jealousy of me," Helen said unhappily.

"Jealousy!" I said, uncomprehending. "Of *you*?"

"Yes," my sister said bravely. "I could feel her jealousy."

Helen was right, of course. Over the years, I benefited from her sensitivities, her genius for seeing truth. Somehow or other, what I absorbed from her from the time I was a small child meshed with my own natural good will, eagerness to please everybody, and buoyant naivety, and the mix turned out to be inestimably valuable for the work I had chosen to do.

But Helen was vulnerable. Like Bill, although she knew how to protect others, she never learned how to protect herself. She was faithful throughout her life to a young man she had loved from the time both were eighteen, but circumstances separated them, and she never recovered. She never realized the considerable promise of her beauty and her talent. It took me years to understand fully how much of her perception and wisdom she had tried so hard to transfer to me. No one but I—not even Bill—could know how much of Helen went into everything I have done. She died in 1971. Bill gave the eulogy at her funeral.

Bill went to college at the University of Michigan, where he elicited exceptional interest from his teachers. He also experienced jealousy on the part of a classmate, and some acute emotions regarding an attractive young woman working in a local delicatessen. His stormy reactions to both experiences drove him to quit college suddenly and run away to the New Mexico town of Las Vegas, where he rented a room and wrote some short stories. He could not sell the stories; he earned his living for several months as a reporter for the town newspaper, the *Las Vegas Daily Optic.*

He returned to Chicago, and the day after his twenty-first birthday, in 1928, he was married to the former Cecille Lyon, a lively and popular features writer at the *Chicago Daily News,* whom he had met when he was seventeen, on a blind date arranged by his cousin Marshall. She was a few years older than Bill. He tried working for the Hearst Pictures Syndicate, as a caption writer. Then, in the spring of 1929, he and his wife went to Europe together by ship. The crossing, he told me, was a disaster for him; he was sick from beginning to end and never left his bed in the stateroom. For most of the time in Europe, he told me, he was sick. He picked up long-lasting flus. He had stomachaches, digestive problems. In Paris, he worked for a while playing the piano in a small bar called La Cloche on the Left Bank. There he felt better. "Paris was to me exactly as it was to everybody else who was there in the 1920s—improbably magical, romantic, unworldly, beautiful," Bill liked to say. "In Paris, you felt immortal." He and his wife made some French friends—heroic people who later worked in the Resistance movement. Bill told me about his complex and strong feelings about one family in particular, the Lemerciers, who became lifelong friends of the Shawns. Mme. Lemercier was a writer and translator, a strong-willed, brilliant, and beautiful woman. During World War II, the elder of her two daughters and her husband were in the Maquis. After the war, Cecille invited the younger Lemercier daughter, Aimée, to come and stay with them, which further strengthened the families' friendship. When Aimée returned to Paris, she married a French newspaper editor. They had a daughter, Marina, who befriended Bill's son Allen when he went to Paris after college to pursue piano studies with Nadia Boulanger. Marina eventually came to the United States, stayed with the Shawns, then went out to California and married a U.S. Navy officer. Bill told me that he and Cecille never wavered in their devotion to the Lemerciers. Bill and his wife stayed in Paris for a few months, and after visiting England and Italy, they returned to Chicago in the late summer of 1929.

In early 1932, Bill came alone to New York. He found a job working for J. C. Penney doing publicity and advertising, but his boss soon told him he didn't understand publicity and advertising and fired him. He tried to write songs, hoping to sell them. It was winter in New York. He was terribly cold all the time. He wore a thin coat that was ragged and ill-fitting. One evening, he walked into the lobby of the Waldorf-Astoria Hotel, thinking he might warm up there. A doorman came over to him and angrily ordered him to leave. Years later, I accompanied Bill to the Waldorf's Peacock Alley lounge to listen to Jimmy Lyon play the piano. Placards all over the hotel urged "Hear Cole Porter's Piano" but did not mention Jimmy Lyon, as though the piano might be playing itself. Bill referred to "the night when I was thrown out of the Waldorf" and joked that perhaps the offending doorman was the same man who had written the copy for the placard eliminating Jimmy Lyon from the playing of Cole Porter's piano. (Bill took lessons in improvisation with Jimmy Lyon for a time.)

In New York, Bill's morale was low, but then some nice things happened. A well-to-do friend from Chicago gave him one of his warm coats. Then Bill discovered, in the Grand Central area, a restaurant called Tessie's, where for twenty-five cents he could get a boiled-beef supper that not only kept him alive but gave him a standard by which he measured all other boiled-beef dishes in subsequent years. Also, Bill loved Tessie, who was feminine and Austrian. (Throughout our years together, Bill often said how much he loved the idea of a small tearoom or café, where one might sit around quietly, perhaps for hours, and read and write or simply think, a place that would feel like Tessie's.) Then Bill fell in with a group that included Aaron Copland and Lehman Engel and some young musicians and songwriters who were, like himself, interested in show business. He began to feel encouraged in his songwriting. Every morning he woke up with new ideas. Melodies rolled over him. He began to feel free of his phobias. But he also began to be aware of certain jealousies and resentments and mean-spiritedness in the group. He played one of his songs for another young songwriter, who then claimed the song as his own. Bill immediately ran away from the group, just as he had run away from the University of Michigan. He abandoned the writing of songs.

In Chicago, there was some family trouble, and Bill was called back. Soon he returned to New York with his wife. *The New Yorker* had begun publication in 1925, and Bill was one of its first readers, one of its first worshipers. He went to the magazine's office in 1933 and obtained an assignment for a report on pickle barrels, for which he would be paid ten dollars. He told me he spent about two weeks at a pickle-barrel factory in New Jersey, getting the information for his report, and two more weeks writing it, but, to his knowledge, the story was never used. He got occasional assignments to do research for stories that would be rewritten by others. He was living at 137 East Fortieth Street at the time, and sporadic payments for his work were mailed to him by Don Wharton, one of Harold Ross's many managing editors.

In a note dated August 30, 1934, the day before Bill's twenty-seventh birthday, Wharton wrote:

> Dear Shawn—
>
> Enclosed find check for $25 for your material on the Roosevelt family genealogy which Frank Sullivan used in his casual "The Roosevelt Family." Thanks for digging this up for us.
>
> Don Wharton

Bill was paid for research on such subjects as Mayor Jimmie Walker's tailor ($27), on Bock Beer ($27), and on old cemeteries ($27).

In 1935, he was given a job in what was then called the Idea Department, and he started coming up with ideas for other people to work on. Harold Ross and St. Clair McKelway, a writer who was also serving for a short period as a managing editor, both started to take notice of Bill, who soon found that he could earn a living by doing for writers what he had done for friends and schoolmates when he was in high school. Often a writer who didn't know what he could do or what was true to himself would be surprised to be given insight and direction by Bill. Then Bill, who had a way of erasing himself from what he was giving, would say to the writer, "Nobody else can do what you can do." He did this work so easily, so smoothly, so quietly, so anonymously, that he could make it seem he wasn't doing anything at all. He could make it seem he wasn't there. He did not have to exist. He did not have to think about existing. Giving his help was a reflex action. It was life-giving—in one way—to lose himself in other creative people. In 1939 he became the managing editor.

On Saturday afternoons, Bill would haunt the Commodore Record Shop and others, listen to jazz records, buy one or two, and then drop in on the British Book Shop, before going home. One Saturday afternoon, he found himself wandering aimlessly near the old Biltmore Hotel by Grand Central Station. "I had a mystical experience," he confided to me. "At the time, a certain young woman was very much in my thoughts. I was going round the corner to the hotel entrance thinking about her, and then, suddenly, she materialized. There she was, just standing there, waiting for a taxi."

"What happened?" I asked. "Did you talk to her? Did you take her into the Biltmore for a drink?"

"I helped her get a taxi," Bill said, blushing and giving the kind of understanding, embarrassed laugh he reserved for himself.

Bill had no interest in acquiring material possessions or in holding on to money; in fact, he seemed to enjoy giving his money away. His habit in tipping a taxi driver was to double the amount on the meter, or on rainy days arbitrarily to triple it. He would fight to get as much money as possible for the people working for him, but it never occurred to him to ask for a raise for himself. He seemed to be driven to do penance eternally. If I expressed strong negative feelings about anyone, friend or stranger, whose conduct I considered execrable, and, further, if I suggested such behavior warranted spikes driven into the head, or worse, Bill's response—even if he had been the one to suffer damage from the wrongdoer—would always be the same: "Everybody is a human being." Then we would have our Hitler dialogue.

"Even Hitler?" I would ask.

"Even Hitler."

Ordinary human instincts of survival were foreign to Bill. His occasional efforts at self-protection were awkward and inept, and puzzling to most others. A few people even accused him of being "devious" or "shrewd." "I have a way of going blank when reality becomes too much for me," he once said to me.

About the time that Bill was securing his place at *The New Yorker,* I was in Syracuse, discovering what the rest of the world, outside of my home, looked like. I played around the tracks of the railroad that went through the middle of the city. With my brother and sister, I would put pennies on the tracks (we didn't know it was illegal) and watch as the trains ran over the pennies. We would stare at the glamorous passengers looking at us through the windows. Then we would collect the flattened, misshapen, marvelously ruined pennies. At Christmastime, after our relocation in the suburbs, when the heavy upstate snow was piled in walls higher than my head along the shoveled walks, I went from house to house in the dark afternoons and evenings selling Christmas Seals. I won prizes for my sales—leather pocketbooks and woolen sweaters—and gave them to my mother. I would be invited inside the brightly decorated homes while the occupants went to get money to pay me. All these homes looked so exotic, so enchanting, so luxurious, and every baby I saw could stand and could walk and could cry. So many happy babies, in high chairs, in cribs, in playpens, in wagons, in the arms of older brothers and sisters. The life I saw in these homes was irresistible. The impact on me was lasting.

After Christmas Seals, I graduated to peddling *Collier's Weekly* magazine, which was the size of, and in competition with, *The Saturday Evening Post. Collier's* rewarded me with prizes of additional pocketbooks and sweaters. The magazine also sent me an official canvas carrying bag, stamped *Collier's,* which I wore strapped over my shoulder. I carried the magazines by the dozens, selling them at a nickel each on the street and to all the neighbors. Again they invited me into their homes, and again I sampled the orderliness, the affluence, the cheeriness of what I later learned were Norman Rockwell people, sprung to life from magazine covers. I fell in love with the fresh-print-and-paper smell of the glossy-covered magazines that I was selling. To this day, every time a fresh issue of *The New Yorker* reaches my hands, the olfactory sense of my early infatuation with magazines immediately takes over. In fact, ever since first grade, when brand-new school books were handed out to me and my fellow students, I have responsed to the pungent, intriguing odor of new books and magazines before reading the first page.

For me, everything about starting school was adventurous. Charles Andrews Elementary and Nottingham Junior High were my temples. I had no phobias. My only obsession (and it is still with me) was with stationery-store supplies—folders, notebooks, colored pencils, and especially paper pads, the little ones with sheets of different colors. As a small child, I slept with an assortment of them under my pillow, compulsively arranged in patterns. It was my sister's bewildering purpose in life, it seemed to me at the time, to muss up the arrangement under my pillow when I wasn't looking.

In school I earned good grades. I always found my teachers interesting. I enjoyed figuring out their personalities, and I was intrigued by their out-of-school lives. Once, in third grade, my teacher, a Miss Hamilton, fat and grim-faced, put me under her desk as punishment for some misbehavior. Under there, I was frightened, but it was *interesting.* Miss Hamilton was wearing big, billowing green bloomers, and I found observing them *very* interesting. Teachers liked me, encouraged me, seemed to be curious about me. In sixth grade I started writing for the school newspaper. My first published story was about the school library. My lead was "Fat books, thin books, tall books, short books..." No byline, but my words were in print. I was overcome by the experience. It was the start of my going in a straight line to what I wanted to do.

When I was in junior high school, my father moved the family to New York City, and I immediately felt the mysterious energy and dramatic appeal of this place that was so wide open and so welcoming and so different from my former silent suburban community in Syracuse. I rejoiced in everything—all that wonderful noisy clatter in the subways, on the streets, in the schools. One way or another, and always with the encouragement of teachers, I kept going, more determined than ever, in the direction of reporting and writing. I never forgot my sister Helen's "traveling correspondent" idea. I now had all the career orientation I would ever need. Wherever I went, in and out of school, I immediately felt the freedom, the acceptance, the joy of New York City. I could feel its welcome to me, to me. The possibilities of the city were overwhelming. All I had to do was get on a subway, ride to Times Square, and walk into buildings.

On a class trip I saw for the first time the composing room of *The New York Times,* where I was immediately seduced by the pungent metallic aromas of the makeup tables and Linotype machines hand operated by wonderful old (it seemed to me) loving men wearing green eyeshades and black-and-white striped aprons. Thereafter I used to return alone to the composing room. I simply walked in, and the green-eyeshaded men would greet me hospitably. They would bestow upon me the magical gift of a lead slug of type with my own name, and I would look upon all of them as my fathers. Time and again, I cut school and went by myself to visit other newspapers and the people who wrote for them. I had discovered that I could just walk in, as long as I looked as though I belonged to somebody there. So I looked in, for one, at the *New York Herald Tribune,* on Lewis Gannett, the book critic. He was delighted to have me stop by unannounced, and then, and thereafter, with an air of complicity about my visits, he regularly gave me piles of new, wonderful-smelling books. I then started reading his reviews. Once, I walked in on F. P. Adams, who wrote a daily column for the paper. He interviewed me as I interviewed him, and in his next day's column he wrote about *me.* My teachers read the column before I knew about it, and they approved of the publicity, so I was spared telling a lie to cover my absence, and I felt encouraged to repeat the performance. I walked into the offices of the *Daily Mirror* and came upon Sidney Fields, a charming example of the traditional newspaperman—slim, with Humphrey Bogart looks and Humphrey Bogart tough talk, hard-drinking and cynical, with a sporty fedora fixed eternally on his head. Joy of joys! Then I discovered Richard Maney and other press agents who were eager to give out passes—to movies, to theatres, to concerts, to museums, to parties. All I had to do was to tell them I worked for the school paper. New York had journalism incarnate, journalism galore. It was an all-encompassing pass to the city. New York was wonderful. New York was glorious. New York was mine. To this day, I have never wanted to live anywhere else.

When I was about fourteen, a friend took me to a party in Greenwich Village that was attended by Henry Miller. At that point, I did not even know that Henry Miller was Henry Miller. (Years later, Norman Mailer explained Henry Miller to me and gave me his books to read.) Miller was sitting on the floor with several other grinning friends. There was no furniture. Everybody was drinking wine and eating chocolate bars. I was horrified. My friend explained to me, in devout tones, that they were Bohemians, poets, intellectuals. To me, they looked unclean and sounded useless and tiresome. I was not drawn to getting down with them, to being a part of that kind of life on the floor. My assumptions for my own life were still those of my parents: a young woman marries a "good man," has healthy children, and leads a modest and useful life. At that point in my experience, I had no problem in reconciling one "good man" with my need to go on with the work I loved. My sister told me that a woman should get married and have her children and *then* do "other things." By that time, I was not taking her advice. My father would have called Henry Miller a "bum" who "took money from women," and that guideline I remained faithful to. As a teenager, I was planning to be a writer and to go out and see the lives of other people in the world, but it never occurred to me to discard my assumptions for my own life. The celebrities—both literary and nonliterary—I might eventually write about never became the people I wanted to model my own life after. In time, at *The New Yorker,* I became aware of a certain sadness and disharmony in the lives, outside the magazine, of some of the writers and artists I most admired. I couldn't make sense of the gap in texture between their personal and their professional lives.

One evening, in the early 1960s, I was walking down Madison Avenue around Sixty-fourth Street, when I recognized an aged Dorothy Parker, walking a tiny dog. I didn't know Dorothy Parker. I didn't try to talk to her. In high school I had read and been strongly affected by her short story "Big

Blonde," and others, and I had enjoyed her light poetry, published in collections. I later learned that she had done book and theatre reviews for *The New Yorker* in the 1920s. Seeing her now, I thought: She was two generations ago! I had heard the legendary, funny anecdotes about her, and like just about everybody else I knew, I had found delight in her work. I had also heard of her drinking, her decline. There she was now, a sad old lady, walking very unsteadily, with a strong alcoholic odor about her. Her hair was unkempt. She had on bedroom slippers and was wearing a shabby housecoat. The expression on her beaten face was one of pain and loneliness and suffering. Seeing her was shattering, frightening. I hurried past her. I told myself it didn't have to be like that. She hadn't done any noticeable writing in so many years. She was of a much *older* era, I told myself. She had even predated Bill Shawn's time there. I was of an entirely different era. For me, it must never be like *that,* never like *that.* One's personal life and professional life, I told myself, could be in line with each other and on the same plane.

I wasn't aware, in my beginnings at *The New Yorker,* of consciously sorting out my feelings about Bill Shawn, but there he was, a sure and solid man, emerging reassuringly into my view on the same high plane—aesthetically and morally and imaginatively and humanely—as everything that mattered to me in whatever I did.

CHAPTER 4

IN THE MEETINGS

Whatever reporting Bill asked me to do turned out to be both challenging and fun. In my first week at *The New Yorker,* Bill asked me to obtain some factual information about the physicist I. I. Rabi, one of the key figures in developing the atomic bomb, to supplement a Profile of him written by Robert Lewis Taylor. So I called on Rabi at his Riverside Drive home, where I found him with a bad head cold. I went out with him to buy a box of Kleenex, a difficult mission, as it turned out, and I hinted in my report that getting a box of tissues was a formidable task for this inventor of the atomic bomb. I also had an early-morning breakfast at the Waldorf with J. Robert Oppenheimer, another key scientist involved in creating the bomb, and I found myself in the alarming position of trying to reassure him and calm him; he was overwrought about his role in building the atomic bomb and was sobbing and saying over and over again "Mea culpa! Mea culpa!" Because I was supposed to be obtaining information about Rabi, I tried to elicit some from Oppenheimer, but he just wanted to talk about how guilty he felt. I wrote all this up, and more, and handed in my report to Bill, who gave me, with his laughter, the reassurance that I needed; he, too, felt the report was simultaneously moving and funny. It gave me a heady feeling: I was making Bill Shawn laugh.

Also, with every new story, I was developing more and more confidence in myself. I knew the purpose of my existence. I didn't have to think about it. Bill told me that my stories were different from those of others. I would know, within the first few minutes of encountering the subject—an individual, an incident, a meeting—exactly what the "story" would be. My enjoyment of the "work" was endless. I would be laughing in anticipation of what I would write. Then Bill would read the story and, laughing, he would praise it.

For me, reporting and writing for the magazine was fun, pure fun. Shortly after I started, for example, Bill told me that a Saudi Arabian prince, Faisal, was in town, and there might be something in his activities for a story for "The Talk of the Town." So I connected with one of Faisal's assistants, Ahmed Abdul Jabbar, a young man who, turned out in a Brooks Brothers suit and turned loose in the city, was having the time of his life doing everything that obedient and proper royal Arabian princes were not supposed to do: drinking, smoking, going to nightclubs, and dancing with beautiful American showgirls. It was O.K., he told me, because Prince Faisal was doing all that too. And he gave me permission to say so in my story, as long as I would write that his favorite song was "I'm the Sheik of Araby, all girls come to me..." He kept on singing it to me and giggling in self-appreciation. Who needed Prince Faisal? I made my Talk story subject Ahmed Abdul Jabbar.

About sixteen months after joining the staff, I saw a newspaper item saying that Kaiser Wilhelm's former yacht was being repaired in a shipyard in Brooklyn. I told Bill I wanted to try writing a "Where Are They Now?" piece about the yacht. Without too much eagerness, he gave me his approval of the idea. "The Kaiser's Yacht" became my first signed piece in the magazine (June 22, 1946). I stayed up half the night, mesmerized, just staring at the words that appeared over my name. The next day, I ran into Harold Ross in the office corridor. He came to an awkward halt.

He said, looking unthrilled, "Shawn says you're not writing Talk anymore."

"Oh, no," I said. "I mean, I still want to write Talk stories."

"You've got to follow your own bent," he said, looking baffled. "Follow your own bent," he repeated, and gave what I took to be his famous grin. I somehow felt encouraged.

Bill went about his job with modesty, speed, diplomacy, courtesy, concentration, and self-effacement. He was hungry for laughter and lightness and originality and all the plain fun, and he was endlessly ingenious and unconventional in grasping my ideas and in giving me his own. Bill's feelings for his writers and artists were akin to love, but his attraction was tuned to their talents.

The diversity of his talented writers and artists never fazed him. He was able to go from one to another with the same high enthusiasm and the same intense focus on each one. He would listen carefully while somebody—articulate or not—tried to explain what he or she wanted to do, and somehow, in some mysterious process of osmosis, he would catch the idea, the original insight, or any one of a hundred possibilities that would lead a creator to come up with a gemlike Talk story, a "Reporter at Large," a Profile, an "Onward and Upward with the Arts," a short or long piece of fiction, an essay, an editorial Comment, a cover, a cartoon. When he discovered a new writer of talent, he was thrilled and happy. If there was no existing department in the magazine to accommodate what a writer wanted to do, Bill would invent one—for instance, "Reflections," for the philosophical Susan Sontag's essays about Antonin Artaud in 1973 and about Roland Barthes in 1982.

Doing Talk was satisfying, but I leapt—with energy and fervor—to the challenge of employing the longer forms. It was never "work" for me. It was fun. I never felt any indecision about my choice. I was in my early twenties. I didn't want anything else the way I wanted to report, to write. I went to parties. I enjoyed nice clothes. I loved watching babies, with whom I have been fascinated since childhood. But I didn't regard my boyfriends as prospective fathers of my possible future babies. And my mental picture of being stuck with this or that particular boyfriend for the rest of my life was distressing. Invariably, I deeply felt that I was alone, but that is how I wanted to be. I felt that I was a normal female, but my passion drove me to being a reporter. I was happy staying on that track.

When I came up with my own ideas for pieces, Bill Shawn, in his inimitable way, would say a few words here and there that somehow gave me the clues to finding new and fresh ways of writing the pieces. Although I did not fully realize it at that point, the two-way conversations I had with Bill Shawn, albeit limited, were the first real two-way conversations I ever had with anybody, including my teachers and my parents and my siblings. It was as though nobody else had ever listened to me before. Bill understood everything I said and the way I said it. I understood everything he said and the way he said it. Through the work, I began to feel that I was not alone. When both Ross and Shawn responded to my writing with enthusiasm, I was more than flattered by their praise; I loved surprising them. Supported by the certain knowledge that they were with me, I was free to be myself in every way and move around to do my reporting. In talking to me, people I was writing about seemed to be responding to my concentrated focus on them, and I didn't have to bother them with me.

Most of the older writers on the staff generously accepted the four young women who had become their colleagues. In fact, they seemed to enjoy having us around. Joe Mitchell, author of the remarkable "McSorley's Wonderful Saloon," and Joe Liebling, who had written pieces as a World War II correspondent, and who now wrote, among other things, the "Wayward Press" department, had also come to the magazine from a newspaper, *The New York World-Telegram,* and they made me feel that I shared that traditional, privileged bond newspaper reporters reserved for one another. When we were chatting at a party once, Joe Mitchell lovingly referred to *The New Yorker* as "our paper." I was transported by the remark. In the physical act of writing, I often didn't know exactly what I was doing; all I knew was that I felt some mystical power moving my fingers over the typewriter keys. Joe Mitchell and I would engage in not quite half-joking discussions of this phenomenon, and we would agree, while laughing at ourselves, that it was real.

A. J. Liebling would take me to lunch, and laughing in that Liebling way that made his body shake like Jell-O, he would nag me about my playing and watching tennis and, even worse (to him), watching baseball. He considered both sports very boring. As his readers knew, he liked boxing and horse racing. As far as I was concerned, Joe & Joe could do no wrong. I was proud of a photograph I took of them together outside on the street of our office building, with Liebling wearing a bowler hat and an English topcoat just barely closed with one button. Liebling used to walk along the corridors with a quizzical expression on his face. It would grow more quizzical whenever he commented on the way I wrote, asking me why I didn't give my opinions, my point of view, in my pieces. It was all said in a good spirit, and I enjoyed his interest, but I didn't want to change my way of reporting and writing. I never thought of asking any other reporter or writer how he did his work; I just assumed that everybody was impelled to do things his own way. If my way of writing was O.K. with Bill Shawn, that was all the confirmation I needed.

Another writer, not on the magazine's staff, who used to reproach me for keeping myself out of my reports was Norman Mailer, before he had begun to write nonfiction as well as fiction. I had written a "Talk of the Town" story about him in 1948, when his first book, *The Naked and the Dead,* was published and became a best-seller. ("Mailer is a good-looking fellow of twenty-five, with blue eyes, big ears, a soft voice, and a forthright manner.... Mailer has an uneasy feeling that Dostoyevsky and Tolstoy, between them, have written everything worth writing, but he nevertheless means to go on turning out novels.") After that, although he told me he didn't think much of my "ear" for his talk, we became friends. I told Bill about the long walks I took with Mailer, and how we told each other what we wanted. I said I wanted to be "the best woman reporter in the world." (It was before women's lib. I was deliberately careful to use the qualifying word "woman.") He said he would be "the best novelist of our time" (no qualification). I felt it would be nice to have his approval. I tried to explain to him that in my view, reporting was at its most effective when the reporter remained unobtrusive. What I tried to do, I said, was to make my point of view implicit in the facts and quotes I used. He seemed to be puzzled by my explanation. Later, he began writing nonfiction of his own design, referring to "Mailer" in the third person. I found his passionate and, as usual, brilliantly written reports original and intriguing, but I had no wish to model my writing after his. (Also, what really mattered to me was that I liked his mother's cooking. She made the best pot roast and potato pancakes I've ever eaten.) When Mailer published his fourth book, *Advertisements for Myself,* I was surprised and flattered to find my name among those he thanked for their support and encouragement. Bill Shawn loved hearing about Mailer and said he'd like to have him write for the magazine. "He's already one of the best writers in the country," Bill said thoughtfully.

I told Norman Mailer I wanted to be "the best woman reporter in the world," and he told me he wanted to be "the best novelist of our time."

At *The New Yorker,* I kept learning and learning from the work of my colleagues. John McCarten, a sweet and endearing man who was always on the verge of self-kidding laughter, would lose his secret miseries in drink, but drunk or sober, he never lost his appetite for humor, and he often taught me how to find the right corner to squeeze a joke into. Geoffrey Hellman, who was tall and elegant and a stylish writer, was said around the office to know "everything about money." In cold weather, he wore a gigantic black fur coat with a large brown sable collar. I told Hellman I had never seen a coat like that except in photographs of old New York in the nineteenth century. Looking pleased, he told me the coat had been handed down to him by his great-grandfather. He lived in a town house in the East Sixties, with his wife, Daphne, a well-known harpist, and their daughter, Daisy. When he heard I needed a place for my clarinet lessons, he gave me the use of his house so that I wouldn't have to disturb the quiet of our office. Philip Hamburger, who, Bill said, had more friends and went to more dinner parties than anybody else he knew, would pop into my office and do funny imitations of people in the news. He was—and still is—the theatre buff *par excellence* (and it is still great fun to hang out with him and his wife, Anna, and listen to their unrestrained ardor for almost everything on a stage). Bill would say that Hamburger should have been a comic actor. I was in a constant state of happiness that these wonderful, inspirational people were my fellow writers.

Harold Ross was appreciative and inspiring. I heard from him directly and also through Bill as managing editor. But it was Bill who was directly in charge of assignments and day-to-day contact. After I started writing Profiles and long reporting pieces, I still wrote short pieces for "The Talk of the Town." I did indeed want to be "the best woman reporter in the world," and I always got a big kick out of competition. Reporting for "The Talk of the Town" made me feel like the quintessential reporter, meeting and conquering the challenge of creating little stories, all factual, that were subtle and telling and funny and true and fresh. That kind of reporting, to this day, reawakens my unyielding, still Linotype-flavored love of journalism.

Bill used to tell me that Katharine White, the fiction editor, was completely dedicated to her fiction writers, and gave them her all. When I ran into her in the ladies' washroom, she always greeted me graciously and unfailingly had some experience of her day to recount. She had the most amazing collection of elegant hats I've ever seen. After I had been at the magazine for about five years, I submitted a story entitled "The Purist Don't Ever Go Crazy." It consisted of a conversation among three young men walking on Broadway near a nightclub called Bop City. Mrs. White returned the story with a note saying: "It was read before it came to me and the votes add up to 'no' I'm sorry to say. I think this one doesn't work out, perhaps because the dialogue doesn't seem natural or funny enough, and perhaps, too, because it all seems to some readers pretty special. I myself think your point of the battle between the purists and 'progressives' and the bop hepcat conventional jazz fan is one that could make a funny piece but to do this special jargon would have to be not too hard going for the layman and the story would have to be very funny, even to the uninitiate. This one seems just a little too tame. Thank you a lot for the manuscript. I'm sorry to be so discouraging." It was a very nice rejection, I thought, and I was impressed by her having really *read* the story. The next time I met her in the ladies' room, she told me a longer-than-usual story about some difficulties she was having with her dentist.

The older writers at *The New Yorker* were almost mythical figures to me. One of my favorites was Wolcott Gibbs. His theatre reviews and other pieces were always the first I turned to in the magazine. In the beginning, I never saw him in the corridors of our office. Other writers told me that he sent in his pieces from home. If Gibbs ever did turn up, and if I were to see him, I was forewarned: "Don't try to make eye contact with him!" my colleagues said. "Above all, do not try to talk to him!"

In 1954, about eight years after I joined the staff of the magazine, I had a tremendous surprise: Wolcott Gibbs talked to me! One afternoon I was sitting in my office when I heard a faint tap on my door. In he walked, a slim, dapper, jaunty-looking fellow, to tell me how greatly he had enjoyed my piece just published in the magazine called "Terrific." It was about young (under-forty) women of the Junior League planning their annual Mardi Gras Ball and, among other items, what to eat at it.

" 'Breast of chicken a darn nice dinner,' " Wolcott Gibbs said, chuckling, and quoting some of my words through his teeth. " 'I move we axe the fruit cup . . . fruit cup is sort of down-beat, partywise.' You really gave it to those bores. I can't abide them," he said, with astonishing ferocity. He stood there for a bit, grinning at me. "Great writing!" he said. Then he left.

I was delighted, of course, to be praised by Wolcott Gibbs, even though I was taken aback by his vehement hostility toward the well-meaning, amiable, good-egg ladies of the Junior League. I had liked all of them and had thought my report on their efforts, although kidding them for their earnestness, was sort of winsome. For a long time, I wondered why Gibbs felt so different about those well-intentioned young ladies. Then Bill one evening mentioned that Wolcott Gibbs, very depressed, had come to see him that day to tell him that he had to go to a wedding in Garden City, Long Island. "He found the prospect absolutely intolerable," Bill said. "He said it was so damn *middle-class.*"

It was only a few years after I came to *The New Yorker* that I set out for Mexico to interview Sidney Franklin, the bullfighter from Brooklyn. It was my own idea, approved by Bill, to do a Profile of him. In 1947, just before Christmas, on my way back from Mexico, I stopped in Hollywood, where I found the motion-picture-industry people trying to cope with the House Un-American Activities Committee. So I decided to write about all that, too.

Then I went to Ketchum, Idaho, to talk to Ernest Hemingway about Sidney Franklin. Franklin had told me about his friendship with Hemingway in Spain in the 1930s and about Hemingway's views of Franklin's bullfighting. ("I may disagree with Ernest, but I'll always give him the benefit of the doubt, because he is a genius," Franklin had said to me, among other things.) The bullfight I went to in Mexico was frightening to me, and I didn't like it, but I was intrigued with Franklin, who was the son of a Brooklyn cop. (Also, I was intrigued with *The Sun Also Rises,* the first Hemingway book I ever read, at the age of nine, when I found it hidden under my brother's pillow in his room.) At any rate, Hemingway and his wife, Mary, were extraordinarily kind to me in Ketchum; they introduced me to the three Hemingway sons, John, Patrick, and Gregory; took me along to Sun Valley Christmas parties hosted by Henry Ford and Averell Harriman; and generously sat me down to a wonderful Christmas dinner cooked by Mary. Hemingway impatiently dismissed Franklin's funny, pompous remarks. ("Ernest got to the point where I knew his mind better than he did himself. It began to annoy him," Franklin had said to me.) Very patiently, Hemingway tried his best to give me an education in the art and meaning and delights of bullfighting. He followed the lesson up with several hopeful, funny, kidding, informative letters to me in New York; in one he said he thought I was "the person least suited in the world to do an article on bullfighting." (He was right, of course.) When I sent him some queries about bullfighting, he replied helpfully and added that he "looked forward with horror" to reading the article. Needless to say, I enjoyed everything he said to me. My piece, "El Único Matador," was a big hit in the magazine. (" 'Death, shmeath, so long as I keep healthy,' Franklin says.") Hemingway later wrote to me from

Hemingway and his wife, Mary, were extraordinarily kind to me in Ketchum. They introduced me to the two younger Hemingway sons, Patrick (left) and Gregory (right); took me along to Sun Valley Christmas parties; and generously sat me down to a wonderful Christmas dinner cooked by Mary.

Venice and said what he called "the Sidney pieces" had got things right and were fine.

Bill, who was constantly thinking of ideas for musical shows, told me he thought "the Sidney pieces" would be the basis for a wonderful and special musical or movie. He suggested that I get in touch with Gene Kelly. Bill was already describing Gene Kelly as Franklin and dance scenes for the bullfighting, and he was starting to compose songs for Kelly and others to sing in the show. So I called up Gene Kelly and told him about the idea. He sent me a telegram saying he was talking to his studio about the possibilities of a screenplay based on the Sidney Franklin profile, and he'd let me know what happened.

What happened? Nothing.

In Hollywood, I met both John Huston and Charlie Chaplin. (In demonstrating to me what he said was appealing to *him* in bullfighting, Chaplin made some graceful, ballet-like veronicas with an invisible cape and said, while his beautiful young wife, Oona, looked on in adoration, "It's a dance, the whole thing is a dance.") Huston had just returned from Washington, where he had appeared before the investigators of "un-Americanism," and he and his wife, Evelyn Keyes, were romantic and intriguing figures to me. They had living with them the seven-year-old Mexican boy, Pablo, whom John had decided to adopt and bring back to the United States. (John had come across Pablo while directing *The Treasure of the Sierra Madre,* the Oscar-winning movie featuring John's father, Walter Huston, and Humphrey Bogart.) John's adventurousness, his singularity, his wildness were magnetically affecting. He was fearless in speaking up about the so-called defenders of Americanism, and sardonic and needling to his colleagues in the movie business who were caving in to the witch-hunting.

In "Come In, Lassie!" I wrote about going to lunch with Huston, then directing *Key Largo,* and his cast—Humphrey Bogart, Lauren Bacall, Edward G. Robinson, and Lionel Barrymore.

Huston was feeling particularly good, because he had just won a battle with the studio to keep in the film some lines from Franklin Roosevelt's message to the Seventy-seventh Congress on January 6, 1942: "But we of the United Nations are not making all this sacrifice of human effort and human lives to return to the kind of world we had after the last world war."

"The big shots wanted Bogie to say this in his own words," Huston explained, "but I insisted that Roosevelt's words were better."

Bogart nodded. "Roosevelt was a good politician," he said. "He could handle those babies in Washington, but they're too smart for guys like me. Hell, I'm no politician. That's what I meant when I said our Washington trip was a mistake."

"Bogie has succeeded in not being a politician," said Huston, who went to Washington with him. "Bogie owns a fifty-four-foot yawl. When you own a fifty-four-foot yawl, you've got to provide for her upkeep."

"The Great Chief died and everybody's guts died with him," Robinson said, looking stern.

"How would you like to see *your* picture on the front page of the Communist paper of Italy?" asked Bogart.

"Nyah," Robinson said, sneering.

"The *Daily Worker* runs Bogie's picture and right away he's a dangerous Communist," said Miss Bacall, who is, as everybody must know, Bogart's wife. "What will happen if the American Legion and the Legion of Decency boycott all his pictures?"

"It's just that my picture in the *Daily Worker* offends me, Baby," said Bogart.

"Nyah," said Robinson.

"Let's eat," said Huston.

Both the Sidney Franklin profile, "El Único Matador," and the satirical Hollywood report, "Come In, Lassie!" elicited a lot of attention, and I was on my way.

My interest in celebrities is always tied to their talent. I find the phenomenon of talent and genius interesting. I've made the mistake, however, of trying to bring a genius together with another genius. The first time, in the 1950s, I brought Joe Mitchell to meet Ernest Hemingway. It seemed logical to me, at that point in my life, to bring the greatest living fiction writer together with the greatest living reporter. Joe had read all of Hemingway's writing. Hemingway had read nothing by Joe. Both men were shy. Hemingway's wife, Mary, broke out champagne, which didn't make for any relaxation. There was stiffness all around. The Hemingways made some talk about a prizefight they had taken me to see the night before. The talk didn't get us onto common ground. I was squirming. Then Mary Hemingway brought in the afternoon newspapers. The headlines were devoted to the scandal of the moment: Ingrid Bergman was having a baby with Roberto Rosselini without benefit of marriage. Hemingway exploded with indignation at the way "Miss Ingrid" was being judged and criticized. And everybody was able to raise a glass to "Miss Ingrid." It wasn't much, but it was something. When Joe and I left, he said, "Wasn't that good, the way Hemingway defended her?" Years later, I wrote about this encounter in *The New Yorker.*

I apparently didn't learn my lesson about what not to do with geniuses. About fifteen years after the Hemingway-Mitchell put-together, I was in Rome, where I had gone to write a profile of Federico Fellini and also a piece about John Huston directing *The Bible* there. I felt called upon to introduce these two magnificent directors to each other, and I arranged a dinner party to be held in a private dining room of a hotel. Both directors came directly from work. Both brought with them a coterie of helpers and hangers-on. The two groups stood at opposite ends of the room, talking with determination only among themselves. As the hostess, I tried to tug Fellini in the direction of Huston, and when I tried to tug at Huston, I let go of Fellini, who retreated. After a while, I pushed them together. Fellini was shy and self-conscious and at a loss for words. He gave a strained smile. Huston, too, was uncomfortable and puzzled. Both men wouldn't talk at all. The entourage of each looked silently at their leader for a cue. No cue was forthcoming. The two geniuses retreated again to their opposite positions. The impasse was my problem. I tried talking about Huston's *The African Queen* and Fellini's *La Dolce Vita.* Nobody cared. Everybody ate with his own entourage. I was thankful that the two geniuses ate and ran.

Before Bill became the editor, while he was still working under Harold Ross, I had firsthand experience with the way Bill exercised his judgment. One of my early long stories, "Symbol of All We Possess," about the Miss America contest in 1949, started out like this: "There are thirteen million women in the United States between the ages of eighteen and twenty-eight. All of them were eligible to compete for the title of Miss America in the annual contest staged in Atlantic City last month if they were high school graduates, were not and had never been married, and were not Negroes." Mr. Ross, in six and a half single-spaced pages of typewritten notes about this piece, questioned my way of pointing up the fact that "Negroes" (the term then in use) were prohibited from participating in the contest. In his notes, he wrote: "I am rather strongly of the opinion that in these days of unrest it would be better not to inject the race problem into this as Miss R. has done—positively instead of negatively. Moreover, this provocative wording is downright misleading—makes reader believe that the point is made here for development later (which it isn't) and is therefore misleading. Could deduct the number of colored maidens and fix unobtrusively as marked." Bill told me about Mr. Ross's query and gave me his notes. I said I thought the lead should stay as written. Bill agreed and published it exactly that way. And Mr. Ross did not object. He had his private prejudices, but he was honest and modest about them, and if he was shown to be wrong, he went along with the correction.

Quite apart from this issue, Ross's notes about my piece (his views on the subject of "colored maidens" notwithstanding) were, and still are, a marvel to me. And they are only one example of the way he went through every piece in every issue of his magazine, questioning the choice of a word, an imprecise impression, a missing fact, and hundreds of other elements in the writing. In these notes, for example, he also wrote: "I don't see why Miss R. doesn't use contractions more than she does—if she does at all: didn't instead of did not. The spelled-out words seem unnatural to me. Have marked in some places. I always feel this way unless the spell-outs are used to indicate character in conversation. People don't talk that way, and, to me, sounds unnatural to write that way in informal writings."

Harold Ross, in my experience with him, was both shy and awkward. Late one afternoon, after I had been at the magazine a few years, he stopped me in the office corridor and said, speaking quickly: "If you'd be interested in having an early dinner at '21' tonight, we could go over there around six, if you'd like to do that."

I was taken aback, but I had no dinner plans, and I had never been to "21," but I had read and heard much about it as a former speakeasy in Prohibition times, and then as a hangout for show-business and literary celebrities. So I said, "I have no dinner plans. I'd be happy to come."

He waved an arm at me. "I've got to eat with Janet Flanner. She'll meet us there. That O.K. with you?"

"Sure," I said. Janet Flanner lived and wrote from Paris, and I had never met her. I had read and admired her pieces, especially a Profile she had written about André Malraux. She seemed to me to be a kind of exotic, eminently knowledgeable, but remote literary figure, sort of like Gertrude Stein. I looked forward to seeing if she was real.

"Meet you at the elevators at six," Mr. Ross said.

We walked over to "21" together, mostly in silence, Mr. Ross setting a fast pace and swinging an overstuffed, well-worn briefcase almost angrily, it seemed, just escaping hitting other people on the sidewalk.

"I don't know of any other place to eat," he said, almost apologetically, as we reached "21."

Janet Flanner was waiting. She had on a heavy gray tweed suit and a black-and-green-striped silk shirt with French cuffs and impressively large black onyx cufflinks. Mr. Ross mumbled an introduction, which Janet Flanner acknowledged with a slight bob of her head. The three of us sat side by side on a banquet with Mr. Ross in the middle. We ordered: scotch and soda, shrimp cocktail, and steak with baked potato for all.

"Janet, did you get to see the art?" Mr. Ross said in a kind of bark, without any preliminary small talk.

"I've seen some of it," she barked back at him, echoing his timbre.

Mr. Ross turned a thumb in her direction and said to me, "She's writing about the art stolen by the Nazis during the war." Then he turned back to her. "I hope you get to see everything, Janet," he said.

They seemed to be very comfortable with each other, like a couple of guys at one of Ross's comfortable poker games. I was having a very good dinner. Otherwise, I didn't know why I was there. Neither one of them paid any further attention to me until the name of Ernest Hemingway came up. I said that I had met Hemingway in Ketchum, Idaho, where I had gone to talk to to him about Sidney Franklin, the bullfighter from Brooklyn about whom I was writing the profile. I said that Hemingway had been very gracious and helpful to me.

"Ernest is a bully," Janet Flanner said.

"Oh no, he—" I began.

"Ernest is a bully!" Janet Flanner said.

That was that. At the end of the dinner, I thanked Mr. Ross.

"The food here isn't bad," he said, with his friendly, crooked grin.

"Ernest is a bully!" Janet Flanner said to me, in parting.

For years thereafter, if I ran into Janet Flanner in our office, she always saluted me by saying, "Ernest is a bully!"

Bill Shawn longed for the freedom to do his own writing. Shortly after I arrived at the magazine, he persuaded Harold Ross to switch his job as managing editor over to the care of Sanderson "Sandy" Vanderbilt, a likable, efficient, if somewhat nervous editor who had been trained under Stanley Walker at the *New York Herald Tribune.* I worked with Sandy, along with the other reporters, and found him very congenial, both as a friend and as an editor. Bill continued at the magazine, in an office directly across from Sandy's, as a "consultant." It turned out that Harold Ross was dissatisfied with the new arrangement, and Sandy was starting to drink heavily. So the arrangement was soon abandoned, and Ross got Bill Shawn to move back into his old office and his old job. Years later, Bill told me that staying on at the magazine had kept him from doing his own writing.

Bill held stubbornly to his own literary taste, his own principles, his own standards. This occasionally put him at odds with writers and editors who didn't share his sensibilities. In 1952, his appointment to Harold Ross's job exacerbated tensions and resentments for a while. Bill was particularly disheartened to hear that James Thurber, who had left the staff of the magazine while Ross was still editor, and who now was experiencing the frustration and pain of blindness, was publicly expressing disapproval of *The New Yorker*'s changes. Thurber talked about Harold Ross's "deep concern about the decline of humor in his magazine" and of Ross's "old dread that the once carefree *New Yorker* was getting into serious areas."

There was no "old dread." Harold Ross had been fully aware of and approved of Shawn's efforts to encourage serious reporting, political and otherwise. The magazine had been getting into serious areas for years, but Shawn's taste and hunger for humor were as strong as ever. "What bothers me editorially is the shortage of humor," he often said to me. "We simply have to be funnier—that is, funny more of the time. And we have to be brilliant more of the time, and we have to be surprising."

Bill Shawn was often at odds with many of the people who perpetuated the basis for widespread resentment of what some regarded as *The New Yorker*'s snobbery, narrow literary focus, and preciousness. Some of Bill's own writers often exhibited a patronizing attitude toward *him*. Bill often felt that he had boxed himself in by his reluctance to oppose people who disagreed with him about his efforts to effect more openness to the world outside of the inbred magazine. They sniffed at his appreciation of, and interest in, for example, certain vital and democratic tendencies in other magazines, which they dubbed "vulgar." Bill sought out talent everywhere and took a lively interest in publications such as *The Village Voice* or *Mother Jones*. He encouraged young reporters and writers for these alternative publications to explore possibilities for their writing for *The New Yorker*. He even watched publications like *Tattler* in England and wondered about its editor, a young, mischievous woman named Tina Brown. No matter what faults or youthful indiscretions characterized these publications, Bill Shawn never dismissed any of them. He knew that they had vitality.

In the late 1940s, Bill and I started moving closer to each other, without any awareness of what was happening between us. As we worked together, we found ourselves laughing a lot and starting to sense what the other was thinking and feeling. One day, Bill introduced me to his wife. The following day he told me thoughtfully that she had said, and Bill agreed, that we had "look-alike faces." Alone, later, I looked in the mirror. Well, I thought, maybe there is indeed a look-alikeness between us. I used to meet Cecille occasionally at parties, where she would do a mean Charleston. I found her to be sensitive and likable and intelligent, with resolute views. She told me that she had been a reporter, but that she had given up working because she felt so strongly that a woman's husband and children demanded undivided time and attention.

One time Bill and Cecille invited me to come up to their apartment on East Ninety-sixth Street; they had heard it was my birthday, and they wanted to celebrate it with a birthday cake. Cecille made a big effort to make the occasion seem natural, but the atmosphere was one of tension and nervousness. It made me wonder what I was doing there. I felt that they were drawing me into their complications. I just wanted to get away from both of them, perhaps out of town, as soon as possible. I began to feel that I somehow might find a way to do the reporting I loved in faraway places.

The idea of writing a Profile of the bullfighter Sidney Franklin gave me a reason immediately to go away. That's when I went to Mexico. I went to bullfights, accompanied Franklin on a harrowing late-night drive from Mexico City to Acapulco, foolishly accepted an invitation from a sinister rich finagler to go on his yacht, saved myself, and learned enough about the bloody killing of bulls to keep me from ever wanting to go to a bullfight again. I oriented my attention fully on being a reporter. I apprised Bill of my adventures in a brief telephone call, leaving out the part about the yacht. Then I went to Hollywood to do the piece about the Un-American Activities Committee's frightening people in the movie business, and to Ketchum, Idaho, near Sun Valley, to ask Ernest

Hemingway about Franklin. I wanted to justify my travels to far-off places by returning with some good stories. I felt I had some lulus, and I returned to New York to do my writing of them. It felt good to be fully back in my reportorial groove.

In 1949, I attended a preview of the Richard Rodgers and Oscar Hammerstein musical *South Pacific* and sat on the aisle next to Joshua Logan, the show's coauthor, coproducer, and director. I reported, in the Talk story I wrote, that Logan started off saying to me, " 'I hope I remember to breathe tonight. I'm always forgetting to breathe on a night like this. Other times, too. Oscar Hammerstein had to keep reminding me to breathe when we were writing the show . . .' "

I reported on Richard Rodgers's conversation at intermission:

> "Josh," he said, "Jake Shubert says it's bringing tears to his eyes."
>
> "Tell Oscar," said Logan.
>
> "Oscar told *me*," Rodgers said.
>
> Oscar Hammerstein appeared and said, "Jake Shubert's laughing."
>
> "I don't dare trust my own senses," Logan said. He took a deep breath and held it, his face slowly darkening.

The story made Bill laugh. He said he wished he had been able to go with me to the preview. He bought a record of the score. Then, over the telephone, he told me how his five-year-old son, Wallace, knew every song on the record by heart.

With every little exchange, there was a deepening of emotional links between us.

Late in 1949, Hemingway asked me to meet him and his wife in New York, where he planned to stop for a couple of days on his way to Europe. By that time, we were real friends, and I wanted to write a Profile about him.

It was Bill who thought of limiting my story to the author's two days and two nights in New York. I had such a good time hanging out with Hemingway and writing about what he said and did—the ride in the taxi from the airport; his talk about New York; his plan to call Marlene Dietrich (whom he affectionately called "the Kraut") as soon as they got to the hotel, after which they would order caviar and champagne; his new book (*Across the River and into the Trees*), the manuscript of which he had brought with him; his visit to a museum and looking at paintings by, among others, his favorite, "Mr. Cezanne"; his shopping for a new coat; his reunion with "the Kraut," and Miss Dietrich's talk, over the caviar and champagne, about living at the Plaza and visiting her daughter and baby grandson on Third Avenue:

> "I'm the baby-sitter. As soon as they leave the house, I go around and look in all the corners and straighten the drawers and clean up. I can't stand a house that isn't neat and clean. I go around in all the corners with towels I bring with me from the Plaza, and I clean up the whole house. Then they come home at one or two in the morning, and I take the dirty towels and some of the baby's things that need washing, and, with my bundle over my shoulder, I go out and get a taxi, and the driver, he thinks I am this old washerwoman from Third Avenue, and he takes me in the taxi and talks to me with sympathy, so I am afraid to let him take me to the Plaza. I get out a block away from the Plaza and I walk home with my bundle and I wash the baby's things, and then I go to sleep."
>
> "Daughter, you're hitting them with the bases loaded," Hemingway said earnestly.

Bill edited the piece, working on it with me at his desk and laughing over and over again at Hemingway's wonderful talk.

> "What I want to be when I am old is a wise old man who won't bore... I'd like to see all the new fighters, horses, ballets, bike

riders, dames, bullfighters, painters, airplanes, sons of bitches, café characters, big international whores, restaurants, years of wine, newsreels, and never have to write a line about any of it.... I'd like to write lots of letters to my friends and get back letters. Would like to be able to make love good until I was eighty-five, the way Clemenceau could. And what I would like to be is not Bernie Baruch. I wouldn't sit on park benches, although I might go around the park once in a while to feed the pigeons, and also I wouldn't have any long beard, so there could be an old man didn't look like Shaw."

Bill and I were both lightheaded with laughter and happiness over the work. Watching Bill's face, in his undisguised joy, free of all his torments, meant more to me than all the praise I later experienced about this piece. The Profile became much talked about for years. In line with the way I like to work, I felt perfectly comfortable in showing it to Ernest Hemingway before it was published, and apparently, he felt perfectly comfortable in making a few suggestions in the interest of accuracy. Also, my friendship with Hemingway and his wife, Mary, went on for years, until they died, he in 1961, and she nine years later. Both wrote letters, funny and informative, about their adventures and misadventures all over the world. On February 9, 1954, they wrote to me from Nairobi, Kenya, where they were taken after their plane crashed while they were flying over the National Park and into the Belgian Congo. They said that they were happy to be alive and that I was practically the first person to let them know that "the United States of America was aware of our adventurous weekend." Hemingway wrote many letters to me from his home in Cuba, the Finca Vigia, and he urged me to come visit and go fishing. I don't like to go fishing, and so I never went there, but I was flattered to be asked.

On May 30, 1950, the day the Hemingway profile, "How Do You like It Now, Gentlemen?," came out in the magazine,

Bill asked me to have lunch with him at the Algonquin. I had been at *The New Yorker* for five years, but this was the first time I was taken to lunch at the Algonquin. It was a heady experience for me, and sitting across from Bill at the table, I grinned at him. He gave me a smile, but I saw that his hands were shaking as he took a sip of water. "It's a wonderful piece, darling," Bill said. He blushed.

I was startled, and I looked startled. He had never addressed me before as "darling."

"It was your idea, to do it that way," I said. Bill did not seem to acknowledge the credit.

"This piece is going to make journalistic history," he said. "After today, you're going to be famous." He seemed to choke back a sob, and he trembled, as I would see him do many times in the years to come.

"I don't need to be famous," I muttered.

"You might go on to other things," he said. "You might go away."

"I don't need to go away," I said.

We sat there, looking at each other, he apparently unable to disguise his feelings, and I, beginning to recognize them but trying not to give a sign that I did. I was in turmoil, but I felt happy.

A couple of months later, that summer, I started finding little poems and messages on my desk, dated and handwritten on our traditional yellow copy paper.

The poems were unexpected and affecting—about meetings and partings. There was the first of many, many poems over the years about circularity. In time, there would be dozens and dozens of poems on occasions such as birthdays, anniversaries, the passage of another year, going away, coming home, Christmas, starting life in our new apartment, and, regularly, about his love. One night when we were working on editing another piece in his office, Bill suddenly blurted out awkwardly that he was in love with me. He told me that I was "beautiful." I tried to pretend I hadn't heard what I had heard and got away as soon as possible.

Alone, later, I examined the facts. I was intrigued by Bill Shawn. He was unique. His youthful energy was endearing. He was appealing, and he was interesting. I admired him, but I had no active interest in life with him outside of the magazine. And I certainly didn't want a consuming relationship with anybody, let alone a man who wasn't free. I knew full well that Bill was married and had three small children; his son Wallace was then five years old, and there were year-old twins, Allen and Mary.

No one had ever uttered the word "beautiful" about me as Bill had. I had never thought, in fact, in terms of "beautiful." I didn't know how to think that way just as I didn't know how to report that way. This was not what I had planned to encounter at this point in my life, in my work. I had never thought of myself as beautiful, quite the contrary. My mind was reeling. Without putting it in so many words to myself, I was beginning to feel connected to him.

At the time, I was going out with an intelligent young doctor, with whom I was sort of marking time in a superficial friendship. It was his dream, he told me, to have a town house in which he would combine his home and his office. I would become discouraged, hearing about the dream, picturing a bunch of sick, demanding patients lining up outside my kitchen and breathing germs on my children, on our dog, and on me. I could admire the life of a dedicated doctor—and the heroic life of a doctor's wife—but I had no wish to make it my life. I wished to go on being a selfish, quiet, dedicated, and free writer.

Without concealing my dismay, I'd express hope that the dream would be fulfilled. The young doctor was being psychoanalyzed, and I tried to pay attention to accounts of his unremarkable adventures with his analyst, who sounded to me like an incompetent and a charlatan. He would harangue the young doctor about his lack of "identity." It also seemed to me that the analyst was encouraging a regrettable tendency in the young doctor to latch on to gossip about celebrated "names" as a way of feeling important and gaining some of that "identity." When I attended parties of his medical friends, I would be simultaneously fascinated and horrified, observing their unhealthy eating patterns (pastrami, pickles, six-layer chocolate cake) and sanitary habits (they never seemed to wash their hands), as well as their gross abuse of the confidential doctor-patient relationship. I liked the young doctor, felt sorry for him, and tried to make a list of his splendid attributes, but I couldn't force them to add up to Mr. Right for me, and I wanted no part of his future.

About ten years later, I used some of my experiences with his medical milieu as a basis for a series of satirical short stories, published in *The New Yorker,* which later became a novel, *Vertical and Horizontal,* featuring Dr. Fifield, the internist, and Dr. Blauberman, the psychoanalyst. It was in this book that I named the heroine Annie because that was the name of Bill's mother. Bill made up the names of other characters, based on the names of old schoolmates and acquaintances in Chicago. It was the first time, Bill told me, laughing, that psychoanalysts had been satirized; most people took them seriously and on their own terms. Bill turned some of the stories over to William Maxwell, head of the fiction department, for editing. Maxwell, a gentle, superb editor, as well as a superior fiction writer himself, surprised me by urging me to go all out in making fun of medical practitioners. We particularly enjoyed one line repeatedly delivered by my fictional Dr. Fifield: "He's a good doctor; he really *wants* his patients to get well." For a couple of years after the book was published, we kept hearing about psychiatric conventions where the chairman would get a big laugh when he started his welcoming address by saying, "Ladies and gentlemen, colleagues, and Dr. Blauberman..." The Chicago journalist Studs Terkel, who played the clarinet, was especially taken with the stories, one of which featured a character named Eephie, a talented clarinetist. Terkel had a radio program, on which he read the story and embellished it by playing his clarinet. So I was, apart from my work, floating around out there, but floating around quite happily and naturally.

And yet, Bill's poems and messages were deeply affecting. But Bill could never leave his wife and children; and, even if he could, I could not stand by for that. I did not want to gain a life on those terms. He agonized over hurting his family, over his sense of distance from them. He was incapable of acting ruthlessly. And if he had been ruthless, I would not have fallen in love with him in the first place. He loved his children. Bill was always supportive of his children in every way. With one exception, he never reproached them for anything, no matter how reprehensible the action, from the time they were infants through their adulthood. The exception, he told me, was when Wallace was in kindergarten and darted between parked cars into the street. Bill, breathless from having run after the child, pulled at his arm and scolded him, briefly, for this scary offense.

Almost every night, at some point, Bill would leave his home, stand across the street from the fifth-floor apartment where I lived at the time, and stare up at my lighted window. Then he would call me from a pay phone to say he was standing there. I was disturbed by all this, and still I was excited by it. We would talk and laugh over the telephone for a long time, and then he would hang up reluctantly and leave. I didn't have enough sophistication or experience with love to understand what might be happening to me. As I said, I have always been less inclined than most people I know to indulge in self-analysis, but I was becoming vaguely conscious of what I was seeing, what I was being touched by, in Bill's face: the purity, the hunger for gaiety and humor, the sadness, the unsettling plea in those clear blue eyes. It was all reaching me, but I wanted to run. But where? I wasn't drawn to reporting in a foreign country. I did indeed still want to be a "traveling correspondent" in the United States. But I loved having New York as my home base; I had no desire to live anywhere else. Meanwhile, the bond drawing me to Bill was becoming stronger and stronger.

The poems continued to appear on my desk.

Bill was giving his writers and artists and the magazine his creative efforts day and night, seven days and seven nights each week. He hardly ever took a vacation. He worked whether he was in the office or at home. In the first few months in 1950, for example, leading up the the publication of the Hemingway Profile, Bill also edited, by himself, an average of four long pieces of writing a week, including an "Annals of Crime" by E. J. Kahn; several "Letters from Paris" by Janet Flanner; a Profile of Ben Sonnenberg by Geoffrey Hellman; a couple of "Letters from Rome" by Janet Flanner; a "Letter from Washington" by Richard Rovere; a Profile of Branch Rickey by Robert Rice; "Horse Racing in Kentucky" by John McNulty; an "Onward and Upward with the Arts" by Thomas Whiteside; a "Footloose" piece about Toscanini by Philip Hamburger; a "Far-Flung Correspondents" piece about Spain by Truman Capote; the three-part "Annals of Crime" by Rebecca West about the Nuremberg Trials; a couple of S. J. Perelman humor pieces; and the weekly Theatre pieces by Wolcott Gibbs. His comprehensive editing, of course, ranged way beyond what "working with a blue pencil" has usually been assumed to mean. It was a complete involvement in the creation of the work, from the beginning of the idea to the development of the theme, the organization of the facts, and the realization of the "story."

The volcanic upheaval in Bill's personal life should have been all-exhausting. Somehow, magically (to use one of his favorite words again), he was able to keep what was professional and what was personal separate. As time went on, all along the line, we found that we could do that. We were guided by common sense. I did not want, did not ask for, and did not receive any preferential treatment. I wanted to be treated like everybody else on the staff. I took great pride in my work and in my certainty that it was judged on its merits.

As the spring went on in 1950, my future was beginning to look muddled, complicated, determined by elements outside my control. I was not unaware of a peculiarly puzzling irony in my situation. I tried not to think much about it, but it kept imposing itself upon me. Bill as my editor seemed to want me to write more and more, but I was in ferment and was losing energy for writing. I've always resisted the intellectualizing with which some people try to diagram their lives. Now I found myself intellectualizing. I would ask myself what I was doing with my life. Why did I seem to be losing my energy for the work I so deeply loved? I tried to stand back from the path I was taking. I tried to figure it out, but I didn't know *how* to figure it out. I wasn't writing enough. I wanted to do more.

As soon as I had been encouraged, a couple of years after joining the staff of the magazine, to try writing longer pieces, in addition to the Talk stories, I had gone at it with fervor. After "El Único Matador," "Come In, Lassie!," and "Symbol of All We Possess," I was on my way, having my say, and getting a glorious response. I followed that with a two-part Profile, "The Millionaire," about Henry Rosenfeld, the most successful dress manufacturer of his day. ("Not long ago, Rosenfeld's chief salesman, a man named Marty Friedman, said, 'If Henry told me, "Marty, go in the middle of Broadway and lay down and let four buses run over you," I would do it for him.' ")

After the Rosenfeld Profile was published, I began to hear from film producers in Hollywood, who held out screenwriting offers to me. I was flattered. Bill looked very serious when I told him about the offers, especially about one from Ray Stark, who wrote that he was coming to New York and asked me to meet him for a drink at the Algonquin. Bill advised me to steer clear of the movie business. "They don't want writers in Hollywood," Bill warned me. "They don't know what to do with real writers." Stark, when I met him, turned out to be a cheerful, polite fellow who looked exceptionally clean and neat in a sporty tweed suit. He was deferential and forthright. He told me that he wanted me to write about his mother-in-law, the comedienne Fanny Brice, who was living at the time with him and his wife in California. My writing, he explained, would then be the basis for a movie, which he would produce. He invited me to come to Hollywood and live in his home, where he would arrange for me to have whatever I needed to work right there in the house. It was a gracious offer, but, as we talked, I knew I didn't want to take him up on it. As an observer, I was drawn to people in the movie business and their work, but I had no wish to be part of it. And to live in somebody else's home? That wasn't for me. Besides, the only writing I wanted to do was for *The New Yorker.* I wasn't influenced by Bill in my decision; I knew I wanted to stay put. I gave an immediate response to Ray Stark, who seemed surprised and yet very sympathetic. (Some years later, a biography of Fanny Brice was published, and eventually, Ray Stark produced *Funny Girl,* first as a Broadway musical and then as a movie, with Barbra Streisand playing Fanny Brice in both. What impressed me was the length of time it had taken Ray Stark to make the movie he had envisioned when he first told me about it.)

With all the attention and praise coming my way, especially after the Hemingway profile, I felt I should have been having a lot of fun. Instead, I was being emotionally distracted and drained.

By midsummer of 1950, I felt desperately that I had to extricate myself from the muddle. I asked for, and received, an assignment to go to Hollywood to write a profile of John Huston, who had become a friend of mine, and who had invited me to come out and watch him make a movie based on Stephen Crane's *The Red Badge of Courage.*

The day before I was scheduled to leave for California, Bill asked me to come to lunch in Bronxville, where he and his family lived for the summer in a rented home. Summers in Bronxville were intolerable to Bill Shawn. He hated to leave New York City. He always felt, he said, that he'd never be able to get back. He once explained to me that he and Cecille rented a furnished home every summer because it was Cecille's "only way of getting a vacation in the country." Bill started out commuting by train, but he soon switched to buying a car and paying a local fireman to drive him to the city every day. If he took an occasional week's "vacation," he would stay put in Bronxville, work on manuscripts, and spend a good part of every day on the telephone talking to writers.

At any rate, I didn't want to visit Bronxville (which I had found previously to be uncomfortably hot and oppressive and irritatingly suburban) for lunch with the Shawns or anybody else. Bill, however, pleaded with me to come up to say goodbye. So I went. We had a pleasant lunch outside on the lawn. Again, however, there was tension. I took photographs of five-year-old Wallace carrying on wildly under the luncheon table and of Bill holding almost-two-year old Allen. In leaving, Bill, holding my arm tightly, walked me down the driveway to my car. He asked me to promise to let him know as soon as I got to Hollywood. I promised. He asked me to write regularly. I promised, feeling self-consciously as though I were being treated like a college-bound kid. He took my hand. His hand was clammy. He was trembling. Cecille, standing back at the house, was calling him. I was nervous and uncomfortable. I didn't want to be there at all, yet I didn't want to act uncaring about him. I found myself feeling sorry for him, but I admired him and loved what he was, and I was incapable of doing or saying anything falsely patronizing about him. I was bewildered. He suddenly kissed me on the mouth and made a hopeless gesture with his arm. I was in a kind of daze. Then I escaped.

CHAPTER 5

LINKED

Immediately upon arriving in Hollywood, I telephoned John Huston and checked in with him. To Cecille, I sent the photographs I had taken in Bronxville of Bill and his family. I arranged to get a car. Then I resolved to keep my mind on what I had come to California to do.

I stayed in Hollywood for a year and a half. Much as I missed New York, I made no return visits to the city. I didn't even return for my brother's wedding. For the first few weeks, Bill and I wrote letters to each other. Mostly, I reported to him about my activities in Hollywood. Then he started telephoning me. Over the telephone, with three thousand miles between us, I felt free to relish talking to him. No tension. No strain. No complications.

As soon as I started telling him about watching the filming, he suggested that I might make something different of the piece; instead of a profile of John Huston, a profile of the movie itself. As I spent time with the characters involved in the making of the picture, I became more and more excited about their relationships with one another, the development of the action, the drama of the story. It was like a novel unraveling right in front of me. It was fact, but it could be fact written in the form of fiction. I would be able to catch it. This was literally thrilling. Eventually, this would become the book *Picture.*

At this point, I wrote Bill a letter, which I came across recently in *The New Yorker Records,* given by the magazine to the New York Public Library Rare Books and Manuscripts Division. It was dated August 12, 1950. I started out telling him, "All this sunshine is not very interesting or stimulating, but so far, that is my major complaint in the two weeks I have been here." I told him that the movie was being shot on Huston's ranch in the San Fernando Valley, and to get there I had to drive seventy miles a day.

"But the kind of story I am getting is certainly worth the rugged life it requires," I wrote. I then told him: "Apart from the movie director side, Huston as a person is almost too interesting to be true—he's complicated, funny, colorful, lonely, generous, crazy, driven, talented and outside of the conventional pattern of Hollywood, yet drawn and held by it, and the people in the business are attracted to and held by him. It's so fascinating to watch that I actually feel at times that I'm not awake. In addition to all this, there is the picture he is making and the way he works, the kind of cast he has assembled for this most-romantic-of-wars war picture—almost all baby faces—and the way he works with them. Now I could limit myself there to the story as a profile, but I am beginning to think there is more in it than that, because there will be the actual making of the picture. It is going to involve so many of the elements of Hollywood that it is too good to let go by.... You see, if the story turns out to be what I think it is, it's really almost a book, a kind of novel-like book because of the way the characters may develop and the variety of relationships that exist among them. I don't know whether this sort of thing has ever been done before, but I don't see why I shouldn't try to do a fact piece in novel form, or maybe a novel in fact form. It's an exciting thing to think about. It's almost as though the subject material calls for that kind of form."

My discovery of how I planned to give my reporting this untried new form was electrifying. I was continually thinking about it. Every time I was around my principal characters in the unfolding drama, I would hear their interchanges in terms of how they would sound in my evolving scenes. I felt as though I were being handed a bonanza. I thought I was the luckiest reporter in the history of journalism. In another letter to Bill, dated September 3, 1950, which I came upon in the New York Public Library, I told him: "If things work out the way I want them to, I will take four characters, Huston, first, then Schary, Reinhardt and Mayer, and tell my story about Hollywood through them, against the background of the industry and in relation to each other. It is the most exciting story to think about that I have ever known."

Bill started telephoning more often. Together, over the telephone, we shared the dramatic events of the movie production, all of it seemingly a story happening just for my writing of it. We had perfect communication. We didn't confine ourselves to the subject of movie-making; we talked about everything. Without realizing what was happening to me, I began to cherish our talk. This man continued to understand every word I said. And I was completely attuned to him. I had never experienced anything like it before with anybody else in my life. I wasn't troubled by the distance. I felt, if anything, closer to Bill than before. It was comfortable and safe, over the telephone.

I informed Bill that I was having a good time in Hollywood, where I made many new friends. I played a lot of tennis and went regularly to tennis afternoons at Charlie and Oona Chaplin's tennis court. Every Sunday, we had delicious tea sandwiches and cakes and drinks served on a terrace overlooking the court. One evening I had an adventurous date

I had followed the making of the picture *The Red Badge of Courage* for M-G-M from the time it started in Hollywood, with John Huston (left) as the director and Gottfried Reinhardt (right) as the producer.

I wrote Bill: "I don't know whether this sort of thing has ever been done before, but I don't see why I shouldn't try to do a fact piece in novel form. . . . It's almost as though the subject material calls for that kind of form."

with Marlon Brando, then acting as Stanley Kowalski in the movie version of *A Streetcar Named Desire.* Brando took me to a Chinese restaurant for dinner, after which we got into our respective cars. He asked me to follow him to the M-G-M parking lot, which was deserted, and he dared me to follow his lead for an hour, which I did, trailing him as he made figure eights. By the time he took me home I was rigid with fear that I might let something get in the way of my primary mission in Hollywood. I could tell that Brando intuitively understood my stiffness, and he gave me friendly laughter in parting. Bill liked hearing about all of it on the telephone.

Humphrey Bogart and his wife, Lauren Bacall, were very kind to me on Christmas Eve, having me over to dinner and to help trim their tree. Bogart sat out most of the trimming, saying it was his option, because it was his birthday, too. "All I do anyway is wait till the end, and then I just throw icicles on it," he said. Another time, Bogart took me along on his fifty-four-foot yawl; he and his crew raced it off Laguna Beach with a bunch of other boats—and lost. I told Bill about it, and he continually wanted to hear more and more about my life in Hollywood.

I went to a lot of parties, given by and for movie people, and I learned that one could have fun in Hollywood as long as one was not dependent on the movie business. I also learned to be partial to great food. I loved to eat in Hollywood. The Chaplins gave wonderful parties. They gave one honoring the second marriage of Carol and Bill Saroyan. Carol—beautiful, brilliant, original, witty, and wise—was sad and regretful as Saroyan chased down girls at the party. (Carol became a lifelong friend, and I was "best lady" at her subsequent marriage, in 1962, to the great actor Walter Matthau at New York's City Hall.) I discovered the patterns of Hollywood life that seem to have remained definitive: the "A," "B," and "C" lists of guests and rooms at big parties; the classic ways of doing business at parties; the elaborate homes; the trophy wives; the necessary jargon; the deep and widespread disappointment and frustration and unhappiness; the fantastic mountains of money; the bad manners; the cloddishness of people in power; the disparity between that cloddishness and the reputations of the clods; and the overwhelming and immeasurable creative talents of the huge majority of capable people in the business, whose prowess and intelligence the people in power call upon to make their movies.

This was a critical time in the history of the motion picture industry: polished young television entrepreneurs, all of them, as I recall, actually wearing dark "suits," were beginning to make themselves heard on the scene, and key players in the movie business were frightened by what they felt was competition. Irving Paul "Swifty" Lazar, the famous, and famously tiny, agent, later wrote me letters—typed on thin baby-blue stationery in lower-case baby-blue type—reporting on the hysteria and depression of people who were fearful of television. When I told Bill about all this, he responded with endless wonder.

For diversion, I hung out with Carol and her closest friend, Oona Chaplin. At a party, I was introduced to S. J. Perelman, the spectacularly clever, one-of-a-kind humorist and satirist, who wrote regularly for *The New Yorker.* He had also written scripts for the Marx Brothers movies. When I read him in *The New Yorker,* his words, so funny and so original, had made me want to turn somersaults and laugh out loud. At the party, he looked like a stern, scholarly professor, with a mustache and steel-rimmed spectacles; he was wearing a handsome Burberry jacket and English waistcoat. Everyone around us was addressing him as Sid. I was thrilled and excited to see him, a real hero. I was introduced to him as a young fellow writer at *The New Yorker* who was out in Hollywood to write a story, or something to that effect. I held out my hand to him. To my surprise, he did not take it. His eyes were the coldest I had ever encountered in my entire life. I felt his resentment at

I wrote to Bill: "You see, if the story turns out to be what I think it is, it's really almost a book, a kind of novel-like book because of the way the characters may develop and the variety of relationships that exist among them." (From left to right: John Huston, Lillian Ross, Audie Murphy.)

"Between you and I and the lamppost," Mayer said, "the smart alecks around here don't know the difference between the heart and the gutter. They don't want to listen to you." (Louis B. Mayer with Lillian Ross.)

I played a lot of tennis and went regularly to tennis afternoons at Charlie and Oona Chaplin's tennis court.

Bogart took me along on his fifty-four-foot yawl, Santana; he and his crew raced it off Laguna Beach with a bunch of other boats and lost.

my being there at all. Then he turned away. I was so numb with shock that it took me quite a while to feel the hurt. I was unprepared for this kind of experience, but it taught me a couple of lessons that I have never forgotten. Lesson one: For years, I had equated humor with the word "human." S. J. Perelman's writing today, decades after his death, can make me laugh out loud, but since getting a good look at him, I have never assumed that a creative artist, no matter how funny, is required to be kind or generous or "human." Lesson two: I have never lost my interest in my younger colleagues (and I've got some mighty talented ones) or my awareness of their sensitivities and their needs. When I told Bill about my encounter with S. J. Perelman, he assured me that Perelman wasn't being "personal." "He's difficult," Bill said, in the dispassionate tone he occasionally strove for in discussing "difficult" people.

Outside the movie business, I met a handsome young scientist who was cerebral and learned, but bitter about the nonprogress of his career. When one came right down to it, he was essentially bitter about life in general. I worked pretty hard to get him to lighten up, but it was tough going. When I played tennis with him, he would become resentful if he lost, and he would accuse me of being "too competitive." So I found myself saying—in a tone I hated to hear in myself—things like "Too com*pet*itive? In *ten*nis?" At that point, I ran to the movie people for relief. And Bill, hearing about this one in detail, was comforting and sympathetic. He was on my side. I felt strongly that Bill was my unshakable friend.

I was also in communication with Harold Ross about the logistical problems of living in Hollywood. I was staying at a hotel, and I considered moving to an apartment to save money. Ross suggested that his friend Dave Chasen, to whom he had lent money with which to start his still famous and successful restaurant, might be able to help me find an apartment. I soon received a "Ross letter."

Dear Lillian:

I monkeyed around and didn't get a letter off to Chasen, so I called up his home yesterday. I was due to call him anyhow, on general principles. I didn't get Chasen, but I got Mrs. Chasen and told her of your wanting an apartment. She immediately told me that rent ceilings have recently been removed out there and that finding apartments is difficult. My wife's sister, who has been staying with my wife and me and is leaving for California today, told me the same thing and, in fact, told me that, with the ceiling off and her children away at school, she intends to rent her house for $1,000,000 a month, or some such.

Mrs. Chasen said that Dave would be useless in this matter but that she knows what's what, and will be glad to help you. You get hold of Dave (if you haven't already) and get in touch with Mrs. Chasen through him.

I hinted to Mrs. Chasen that you should be given a break on restaurant prices. All I can do is hint.

Let me know what happens out there.

As ever,
H. W. Ross

Bill was now making his calls from New York later and later in the evening, and we stayed on the telephone longer and longer. Once he called to tell me that his son Wallace had just had an emergency appendectomy, and he described how tiny and pale the little boy looked in the large hospital bed. During another call, he told me his name had been put up for membership in a prestigious club, but that he didn't believe in prestigious clubs, so he had to figure out a way of graciously getting out of the membership. Every time, as the years went on, he was offered a prize, an award, an honorary degree, he would tell me how he was going to avoid receiving it. Or he would say he was going to send someone else in his place to accept the prize. Over the years, among the honorary degrees he turned down were those from Harvard, Yale, Princeton, Cornell, Columbia, and Michigan, which he had left as an undergraduate.

I returned to New York in late November of 1951 to finish writing my movie story. In California, my high energy for reporting and writing had returned. The friendships I had formed in Hollywood—with Oona and Charlie Chaplin, with Carol Saroyan, and with all of the key figures I had come to know throughout the filming of *The Red Badge of Courage,* especially the Gottfried Reinhardts and John Huston and his wife, Ricki (mother of Anjelica, Tony, and Allegra Huston), would become steady and lasting. I was free and untroubled. My relationship with Bill had been confined to the telephone. Over the past year and a half, we had joked and laughed and talked about our casual lives, but he had made no reference to being in love with me.

When I was in Hollywood I had heard that Harold Ross had been ill, but no one, including Bill, said anything about his being seriously ill, and the news of his death, early in December 1951, came as a shock. At the memorial service, held at the Frank Campbell Funeral Home, Bill greeted staff members and others in a kind of daze. When he saw me, he looked desperate, almost angry. For the next few weeks, the corridors of our office were still. I stayed in my own office for the most part, still working on the Hollywood story. When I ran into my colleagues, they voiced concerns about who might be named the next editor. Almost everybody I talked to felt as I did: How could it be anybody but Bill? Some of the older writers suggested that Katharine White or Gus Lobrano, the fiction editors, wanted the job. *Fiction* editors? "Impossible," said Joe Liebling. "Impossible," said Joe Mitchell. They said it had to be someone who would know how to continue the great tradition of factual reporting and writing.

In late January 1952, William Shawn was named the new editor. It just seemed so logical to us; it was no surprise. Bill stopped in at my office. I congratulated him. He looked thoughtful, somewhat absent, the way I was to see him look while playing George Gershwin. At that point, I was making no connection between his confidences about his "secret self" and having him in charge of the magazine—a great bonanza for writers, including me. Like my colleagues, I took his being editor-in-chief for granted. Because I wanted him to be the editor-in-chief, ergo, he should be the editor-in-chief. But I noticed the absence of joy in him. Yet he gave no sign of what the "secret self" in him was feeling. He just seemed very sober, even numb.

Along with everybody I admired at the magazine, I was thinking only of how great it was to have him in the job. It never occurred to me to wonder if he wanted it.

Some years down the line, he would tell me that Harold Ross had repeatedly brought up the subject of succession, saying that he was the only other person capable of being the magazine's editor. Later, of course, I understood that having been told that by Harold Ross immediately made him feel he had no choice. That's all there was to it. It made no difference that Harold Ross had said something quite different to him before he went to Boston for the operation he never came out of: "He begged me not to try to go on with the magazine, because, he said, 'It will kill you,' " Bill recalled. And, indeed, he sometimes felt that it might. Then Bill told me that what he really felt was that he was trapped, forever trapped, in what seemed to him was nonexistence. Why, then, had he taken the job? I asked him.

"There was no one else who could have kept the magazine alive," he said. "I could not abandon all those people. I could not do it."

From time to time, Cecille and I would find ourselves at the same party—for instance, one E. B. White and his wife,

Katharine, gave for Bill when he was named editor. At the Whites' party, Cecille talked to Katharine White, while I fell in with the cartoonist Peter Arno, a very handsome man, it seemed to me. He asked me if he might take me home. I accepted. But Bill moved in on us, whispering to me that Arno was "dangerous." And so I found myself being escorted home by Bill and Cecille together!

I felt free of any personal entanglement with Bill when I sat down with him to consider how to finish my story about the making of a Hollywood movie.

As we worked on the story, he came up with inspired ideas, especially for the ending, which takes place in New York City. He insisted that I had to report one last element. I had followed the making of the picture from the start, in Hollywood, when John Huston, the director, and Gottfried Reinhardt, the producer, wanted to make it for M-G-M. At the beginning of the story, I wrote: "I decided to follow the history of that particular movie from beginning to end, in order to learn whatever I might learn about the American motion-picture industry." Louis B. Mayer, whose title was vice-president in charge of the studio, was against making the picture, because he did not think it would make money. Dore Schary, the M-G-M vice-president in charge of production, wanted to make the picture. Nicholas B. Schenck, the president of M-G-M, ran the company from his office in New York, and, it turned out, he had given the green light to Huston and Reinhardt to make the picture. L. B. Mayer was furious; he favored Andy Hardy–type movies starring Mickey Rooney. It also turned out that Mayer and Schenck were engaged in a power struggle. In reporting the story, I was able to show who was doing what to whom and why, all the way up to Schenck's office. But I had not been able to see Schenck himself. His press representative, Howard Dietz (who was also a songwriter), was getting in my way. Bill, with aggressive *Front Page* command, said I had to get to Nicholas Schenck for the ending to my tale. He urged me to go to the building at 1540 Broadway where Schenck had maintained his office for the past thirty years, and, starting a vigil at eight o'clock in the morning, wait for him to show up. ("Roseanne *Smith* didn't have a police press pass!") Sure enough, on my first eight A.M. try, a chauffeured car pulled up, and Nicholas Schenck stepped out. I introduced myself, explained that I had been following the fate of *The Red Badge of Courage* from the time it had started in production, and told him that I needed to talk to him for the ending to my story. He graciously invited me to accompany him upstairs to his office. There, to my reportorial delight, with Howard Dietz sitting with us to supply the back-and-forth dialogue, Nicholas Schenck gave me the novelistic scene I needed.

> " 'Red Badge' had no stars and no story," said Dietz. "It wasn't any good."
>
> "They did the best they could with it," said Schenck. "Unfortunately, that sort of thing costs money. If you don't spend money, you never learn." He laughed knowingly. "After the picture was made, Louie didn't want to release it," he said. "Louie said that as long as he was head of the studio, the picture would never be released. He refused to release it, but I changed *that*."
>
> Schenck puffed quickly on his cigarette. "How else was I going to teach Dore?" he said. "I supported Dore. I let him make the picture. I knew that the best way to help him was to let him make a mistake. Now he will know better. A young man has to learn by making mistakes. I don't think he'll want to make a picture like that again..."

When the story, "Production Number 1512," came out, over a five week period (5/24/52–6/21/52), Bill and I heard, the magazine sold out on the newstands in Hollywood as soon as it appeared. Then the series was published as the book *Pic-*

ture (Bill's title), which garnered widespread praise as something special. Ernest Hemingway wrote to me, saying he had sent my publisher a quote for the dust jacket: "Much better than most novels." For the English edition, I had praise from Sir Alexander Korda ("Wonderful. I always knew that the world in which I live and work is mad—funny and tragic—glamorous and sordid—hysterical and sober: and Lillian Ross's acid, though it may hurt all us film people, makes us laugh about ourselves too") and from Graham Greene ("A terrifying picture of how a great film, directed by one of the best living directors, based on an American classic, can be slashed into incoherence through the timidities and the illiteracy of studio heads").

Somewhere along the line, a critic made up the phrase "fly on the wall," to describe my journalistic "technique." Bill called it "a silly and meaningless phrase." He said, "It's for people who don't understand that every writer is different from every other writer, the way every human being is different from every other." *Picture* has been republished many times over the years and is currently available in a Modern Library edition. I had told Bill that I wanted to dedicate the book to him, but he urged me to dedicate it to the magazine instead, so I did that. Bill wrote the jacket copy, in which he said, "The story, while wholly factual, takes the form of a novel." It was something new in journalism, and this was the first time that the concept had been defined.

In Hollywood I had learned how to give a Hollywood party. So—ensconced in the East Seventy-sixth Street three-room, white-floored, white-walled, white-fixtured walk-up I was renting from Carol Saroyan—it wasn't too long before I gave a Hollywood party. It was for Oona and Charlie Chaplin, in the fall of 1952, in honor of the opening of his movie *Limelight,* produced and directed by him and starring him as an aging music hall entertainer. I invited Joe Mitchell and his wife, Therese, and William Shawn and his wife, Cecille, and

Oona's brother Sean O'Neil, and my brother, Simeon, and his wife, Estelle, together with my sister Helen, Oona's mother, and an assortment of Hollywood celebrities, including Gottfried Reinhardt and his wife, Silvia. (John Huston was in Africa, making *The African Queen.* His wife, Ricki, was back in California, taking care of her babies, Tony and Anjelica.) I had the usual round tables seating six each in the living room, foyer, and bedroom and great Hollywood-party-type food. Even "Swifty" Lazar called up and invited himself, in the great Hollywood tradition, to the party (and came). Cecille sat on the sofa with Oona, discussing children, and graciously offered to make her small children, Wallace and Allen, available to play with the Chaplins' three children, Geraldine, Michael, and Josephine. Bill reminded Charlie that at the age of sixteen he had come to see Charlie, at the time stopping in Chicago, and had asked him if he might write his biography. Charlie, giving Bill his kindly *Limelight* look, said he didn't remember the visit, and the two men had a good laugh about that. Everybody enjoyed my party, and I was made to feel like a successful Hollywood hostess. I had a good time telling Carol all about it on the telephone.

Then poems and messages from Bill began again to appear on my desk. Once again I was frightened.

He was spelling it out for me. And he was again showing me that he felt he was sinking into oblivion. It was difficult for me to understand his misery. This was a period, after all, that coincided with his creation of some of the most brilliant, spectacular, and significant journalism in history. And his magazine, however often it was attacked for its outspokenness, was also being applauded all over the world. Years later, he told me that he did not experience all this as pleasure; it brought him no happiness. However, it began to be easier for me than for most others to separate him from his work. He would look solemnly at me, hiding nothing of his despair, and

I began to absorb the realization that he had to be the person he was. I knew that what he was feeling was real. Responsible as he was toward the magazine and the lives of all the creative people involved with it, attuned as he made himself to all their frailties and disappointments and successes and joys, he could do nothing to help himself. He wanted someone to know and believe there was more to him; he was desperate to feel alive. And that responsibility was somehow, mysteriously, becoming mine.

One day I was in my office, reading my New York *Daily News,* when Bill appeared. We looked at each other. It was late morning. Neither of us spoke. We went outside, got into a taxi, and, still without a word, went directly to the Plaza Hotel, got a pretty room, went to bed and stayed there for the rest of the day and evening. Everything between us was so natural, so easy, there wasn't anything to say about it. It seemed that we had been together for years.

Nevertheless, it was impossible to ignore the question of what to do. I had no experience with this kind of trouble. We talked about what happens in a marriage when the parties start being hurtful to each other, in effect, on a path leading to mutual destruction. We talked about what happens to children in a home when they are told lies to explain parental absences. We agreed that children always know the truth, and when they are told lies, they invariably feel that the trouble is their fault. Bill said that he could not unilaterally tell his children the truth, and he was resigned to the fact that his children would grow up in an atmosphere of untruth.

When I was with Bill, I was happy. He was happy being with me. Then I would have hours or days of despair, and I would tell him that I didn't know if I could go on with what felt like a dishonesty. But we had no arguments with each other about the course we were following, because there was absolutely nothing to argue about. I agreed that he could not leave Cecille. He said that his real self was not in his home. He said that his presence in his home was a deception, that he made efforts to be with his children, but that he felt like a failure with them. Cecille, he said, wanted him to be sitting there no matter what. If I left him, he said, it would change nothing in his home. If I left him, he literally could not live, he said. I believed everything he said. Bill never lied. He was no philanderer. He was no scoundrel. He was Bill. I made a conscious decision to try to stay with him, but my feelings seesawed up and down. Instead of working, I would be on the seesaw.

He could not alter his course, but over time he made it equally plain that he was unable to alter his course with me. He took complete responsibility for what was happening, yet he felt that if he and Cecille were to stay married, then her involvement in all our logistical adjustments was inevitable. I accepted the course he outlined: invisibly and intangibly, it would be necessary for her to take part in our arrangements.

For a while, we put our life together out of reach of everybody else. We were so happy to be together that we put thoughts about problems on hold. My love for this man pervaded my entire being. It was extraordinary, because we had indeed become one. Whatever I did in the way of writing was simply a part of him, but only a part. The quality and certainty of our multilevel friendship became stronger by the day. It was not a matter of his making a declaration and my blindly following, but rather of a recognition within me that his feelings were mine, that I wanted this too.

Was I a dope? Was there a vacancy in me? Why was I not beset with guilt—or with resentment—about the woman who remained Bill's wife? Why didn't I react with anger toward a man who did not move decisively to obtain his freedom from a marriage that, he told me, did not give him the life he wanted? Why didn't I act decisively, for that matter, and issue him an ultimatum?

Neither of us acted in these well-worn ways because we weren't adversaries; we were lovers. We were unable to solve our problems, although we persisted in asking each other most of the unanswerable questions. I wouldn't be spared rage or disappointment from time to time, but never, not for a moment, did I feel humiliation or pain. Bill suffered depression, guilt, and pain alone. In some superhuman way, he made it impossible for me to be drawn into those areas with him. Also, he made it clear that the difficulties in his marriage preceded me and had nothing to do with me. Even now, the sadness of it is difficult to state, because Cecille—no matter how involved she had to be in deciding the hours and days of our life—was in truth *outside* of us.

At times, however, when Bill would leave me to check in a few blocks north, anger would rise in me. Why? I wasn't lonely. I didn't feel abandoned. I wasn't embarrassed. I was happy. But I was going against those ingrained family precepts: A woman finds a good man, gets married, has a home, and has children. That was it. But it wasn't all of it. What I didn't say definitively to myself was that I didn't seem able to get fully back to my first love: reporting. And who was stopping me? Not Bill. I was stopping myself. So every once in a while, I would explode. I would ask him to leave me alone, let me be. If he loved me, I would say, he should let me be. I would ask him not to call me anymore. I was enjoying my life before he told me he loved me. I said everything people in my position say. He would go pale, tremble, and agree. We would wait a day, occasionally a couple of days. Then one of us would call the other, or he would show up. And we would be together again.

Something else was also beginning to take place. He was changing me. I was already absorbing some of his nature, his character, his spirit. I was unable to feel anger or resentment toward Cecille; I felt only sorrow.

Bill and I could not stay away from each other. He had an eye for what was beautiful, a word I had previously had difficulty with, so I rarely used it. I wanted to understand what he saw as beautiful—a house, a painting, a color, a child, a woman—and he was able to give me definitions. I was then able to use the word "beautiful," as if for the first time. He constantly used the word about me. I would think about the very first time that a boy on a date told me I was "beautiful." I was thirteen, and we were at a New Year's night performance of *Porgy and Bess.* In my family, I was the "cute" one; my sister was "beautiful." These were *facts.* I didn't question them. My puzzled report to my sister about the date brought forth laughter, innocent laughter, including my own. After all those years, I was becoming receptive to, and deeply affected by, being called beautiful. And I was beginning to understand what it meant.

Whether I realized it or not, the bond between Bill and me was becoming unbreakable. We would talk about separating. I would tell Bill I didn't want to be the cause of pain to Cecille. Bill would say our love had a life of its own, and that I was not the cause of the trouble in his marriage. Then he would say that our attempts to control what was happening to us—our intellectually arrived-at resolutions—came to nothing. We had to be together, in spite of the painful circumstances, he would say. We seemed to have no choice. Our feelings were relentlessly decisive.

Up to that point in my life, my feelings had never been greatly bruised by any big betrayals or assaults. I had never experienced overwhelming frustrations. I never seemed to envy other people (with the possible exception of better tennis players). I had encountered some resentments and jealousies and occasional cruelties, but I had seemed to get through the problems with minimal damage. I had got through family crises, tragedies, illnesses, and deaths. Still, I was aware of having had, before my engagement with Bill, a constant longing for serenity and quiet. Now Bill was raising the comfort level of my entire being to extraordinary heights. But where was my serenity?

One of my sophisticated friends occasionally entertained me by singing a blues song with a lyric that went: "Death doesn't scare me, it's livin' without my man makes me crazy." The truth, however, was that I never felt I really was "livin' without my man." He might go ten blocks north, I might go thousands of miles in any direction, but I never could feel that I missed him. He was always with me. We were always together. Even when I would back away from him, go away from him, run away, tell him not to call me anymore, tell him to leave me alone, I felt I couldn't leave him, any more than he could leave me. The very first moment I looked into his face, the day I met him in his office, I recognized the honesty in it and the familiarity. I must have known then that it was the face of "my man." When he told me he loved me, how was I supposed to go on "livin' without my man"?

And yet. And yet. Life with Bill was not the life I was supposed to have. I kept coming back to the paradox of my situation. Bill, as my editor, seemed to want me to write more; yet the more engulfed I became in our life, the less I wrote. I tried not to dwell on this, but it kept imposing itself on me. I loved this man. I wanted to give him everything, but I missed the writing; I didn't have my old energy for the work. I was unable to formulate a discomfiting thought: that maybe when you love someone, you don't want to admit to yourself that there could be even a small destructive element in the relationship.

I was playing tennis every morning, going home to shower and dress, and then meeting Bill for breakfast. We would meet again for lunch and then for supper. He would drop me at home and return in time to watch the eleven o'clock evening news on television and then, at eleven-thirty, *The Saint*. We would go to a great restaurant some nights, then go to the theatre or a movie, or to a club to listen to some jazz. We spent every Saturday together. I seemed always to be fighting for time to concentrate on a Profile I was doing—of Harry Winston, the diamond merchant. I might write a "Talk of the Town" story. But I was keenly aware of a change in me.

Something was missing: I was no longer hell-bent on becoming "the best woman reporter in the world." And leading this wondrous life with Bill, strangely, seemed to be driving me not to write, but to have other wants, especially a child.

I couldn't reconcile myself to being a "mistress." I didn't *feel* like one. Bill told me I was his "wife." I felt I was. He told me over and over again of his guilt and distress in his home with his wife. He repeated: "I am there but not there." Everything he said felt true. In actuality, I didn't mind not sleeping through a long night with him. But I could not accept living in a framework of dishonesty. I told myself that I could not do it.

In 1953, I ran away from it again.

I went alone to Paris. I felt I had to make the biggest effort of my life to separate from Bill. When I checked into my hotel, I found a telegram there from him, saying he wanted me to enjoy that "loveliest of all cities" and to imagine he was there with me.

The next day, I had a telephone call from him, asking me not to stay away too long and not to let anything happen to keep us apart longer than necessary.

For the next week or so, I had some kind of flu and stayed in my hotel room. Telephone circuits in 1953 would frustrate us, so after reaching me on the telephone, he would send a cable, saying he was worried and admonishing me to stay in bed, drink liquids, and be watched by a "good" doctor. He cabled me to cable him about how I felt. He cabled to inform me when he would telephone. When one has the flu, alone in a hotel room in Paris, that kind of attention doesn't feel excessive.

I couldn't help loving his inimitable cables, and I couldn't help enjoying his inimitable telephone calls. On the other hand, I tried to hold to my resolve to break away. I focused on getting back to work. I wanted to write about who was left in the way of "royalty" in Europe. I wanted to finish writing my Profile of Harry Winston. To all this, Bill responded with encouragement in his cables and in his calls, but the encouragement to work was interwoven with an implicit assumption that I was "away" but not "separate" from him.

Over the telephone, Bill asked me to look up some of his haunts from the 1929 trip with Cecille, which had been his first and only visit to Europe. He even urged me to visit Aimée Lemercier and her husband in Paris, which I did, and I had a delicious dinner cooked by her mother, Mme. Lemercier. During the dinner, Aimée told me that I "acted and talked" just like Bill and had his rhythms—which I was not aware of. (Thereafter, as time went on, I caught myself occasionally acting and talking like Bill, but laughing at myself, I cured myself of it. Nevertheless, as so often happens with a couple in love, I naturally and proudly absorbed some of his vocabulary and subtly tried to appropriate his patterns of politeness. In fact, I noticed that some of my colleagues who were sensitive to Bill also took on his special vocabulary.)

I asked myself why he wanted me to retrace his visit with his wife a quarter of a century earlier. I couldn't make any sense of it. Why was I doing it? I didn't know. Maybe I had nothing better to do in Paris. And maybe I wanted him to be there with me. I simply didn't know. It wasn't something to think about. It was something to do. He asked me to go to the Café aux Deux Magots on the Boulevard St.-Germain and to go across the street, to St.-Germain-des-Pres, where he used to sit in the little churchyard on a bench. It was a place, he said, where he used to go to think about the novels he was going to write before he was forty-six years old. In 1953, he was just forty-six years old.

So I marched around the Left Bank, finding and taking photographs of every place he asked me to visit, everything he asked me to look at. "Go to the rue Jacob," he said to me.

"Find a tiny, ancient hotel. Number 44. It will be the Hôtel Jacob." I found it and photographed it. It was now called the Hôtel d'Angleterre. "Find a restaurant called La Cloche on the rue Jacob," he said. "On the ground floor was the restaurant proper, and downstairs was a bar, and in the back room of the bar was a piano I played. Go there and look at it for both of us." (Some separation!) I found a restaurant called La Petite Chaise, which used to be called La Cloche, near the rue Jacob, not on it, and photographed it and ate in it. The food was exquisite, but the bar downstairs had been turned into a storeroom, and the piano was gone.

Bill would telephone and say we "were making the rounds together." I went to 196 boulevard St.-Germain to find his favorite patisserie, with little tables and "astonishing" pastries. I sat there, ate pastries, and realized he had mentioned the patisserie after telling me that an office boy had just brought him his lunch—a peanut-butter sandwich and a vanilla milkshake.

As I followed Bill's directions, going from place to place, I thought about Bill and his wife a quarter of a century earlier. At first, this made me feel ridiculous. Why should I care where they had sat, where they had walked, where they had slept? What am *I* doing, and why am I doing it? I asked myself. I had to detach myself from Bill Shawn. But then I began to realize that it was his past, part of him, and I began to respond naturally to sharing it. I went dutifully about the business of retracing his steps. I took photographs of all of Bill's places and sent them to him. He replied by telling me he had nothing to send in exchange but his love, and he urged me to come back soon. How could I detach myself from that?

I wasn't able to think philosophically at the time about my acceptance of this turning over of my own life to someone else. All I can remember is that it felt natural. One can't change history, and one can't destroy it, so the acceptance of it just naturally becomes part of oneself. However, while accepting it, I tried to resist accepting it. "I am there, but I am not there," Bill continued to say to me about his marriage, about his life. I thought about how fed up I was with listening to this about his marriage. That was not my concern. That, as I have said, was an abstraction. I thought about how he looked when he came from "there," how I would cringe, looking at him. It was so upsetting to see his face revealing the way he was being punished—"Every morning and every night I am there, as though it's the first day," he would say—but I felt helpless to change that situation. I was thinking about myself. I wanted a different kind of life. This one was in disarray. Why had he become my responsibility?

I tried to make myself intent on separation. Then Bill had difficulty getting his calls through. Instead of trying to call me from his office, he would go to the telephone booths of Grand Central Station, where operators at the time would try to place international calls. There, he was thought by the operators to be a mysterious millionaire in love with a French ballerina. They were disappointed when he was disappointed, he told me.

From Paris, I went to Vevey, Switzerland, where I stayed in a hotel overlooking Lake Leman. I worked at getting my energy back. I took long walks along Lake Leman, thinking about the piece I was working on—about Harry Winston, who loved his diamonds as his children. ("Winston sat down and looked at the stone through his loupe. 'The child is healthy,' he said.") I found it difficult to concentrate. My mind would go to Bill. How could we go on talking over the staticky telephone? One morning, he got through to me, saying he longed to be there with me, away from the "uncomprehending" world. I tried to keep my mind on Harry Winston and his diamonds.

I visited Charlie and Oona Chaplin, who, having been prohibited by our Communist-fearing State Department from reentering the United States after a European trip (they left the United States a few days after my "Hollywood" party), had bought and moved into a large *manoir* in Corsier-sur-

Vevey, near Lausanne. Their new home had beautiful grounds and a tennis court. The Chaplins insisted that I come to dinner regularly, and I enjoyed being there—playing tennis, watching their beautiful small children, dining with them and their friends, and eating good food—especially after a concentrated day of writing.

At dinner one night at the Chaplins', I met Truman Capote, visiting with his friend Jack Dunphy. Capote entertained the Chaplins with gossip and funny parodies and acerbic characterizations of people they all knew. He was ingratiating. For some reason, he was able to make everybody, including me, laugh at what should have been shocking—for example, his imitation of the blind Helen Keller visiting the White House. He was very curious about the way I had written *Picture* and questioned me extensively about how I took notes, how much I used of what I heard, and so forth. I had never before been questioned so thoroughly about the mechanics of my reporting, and I tried to explain to Capote that the mechanics were irrelevant. The key elements, I told him, were the characters, their interaction with one another, and the background and dramatic developments in their situation. I told him about my excitement at having discovered the power of factual writing in fictional form. I told him how much more difficult it was to use only observable facts in this form, but that I thoroughly enjoyed that challenge. You must never arrogate to yourself the right to say what your characters are thinking or feeling, I told him; you have to demonstrate all that from the outside, in what they say and do. I was flattered to see him take notes on everything I said.

(In New York, over the next ten years or so, when I would run into Capote, he always wanted to talk about what he called "reportage" and I preferred to call "reporting." He was living in the stage designer Oliver Smith's house in Brooklyn for a while and wanted me to come to dinner there to talk again about "reportage," but I couldn't make it out there. One evening, however, when I was visiting Carol and Walter Matthau at their Upper East Side apartment, Capote turned up, said he had just come from a brutal session with his dentist and needed a martini, expressed shock at the unavailability of the drink, went out and procured the makings of martinis, and gave me a couple of the drinks. Thus encouraged, I talked my head off about my love of "reporting.")

On another occasion an attractive but somewhat beaten-looking woman arrived at the Chaplins' door unannounced. Chaplin's welcome to her was enthusiastic, but Oona's was much less so. It turned out that the woman was an old friend of Charlie's. She was clearly in some kind of deep emotional trouble and was worrying about how to find help. So Charlie, taking a deep breath, and standing before her in a dramatic pose, delivered the "You must live!" speech, word for word, that he gives, in his movie *Limelight*, as the character of the elderly entertainer to the sad young dancer who can no longer walk, let alone dance. The troubled visitor then left, looking puzzled.

Each night on my return to the hotel, I would get a call from Bill. He said the days for him were now "a dragging torture." Except for the times we were on the phone together, he said, all was dark, but he was asking me to go on with him because he knew in his heart that our love could and would survive anything. It was becoming clear to me that the circumstances of our life together would be formidable whether we went on or not. The logical and moral answers in our predicament were sound, but we weren't able to follow them. I knew in my heart that we truly loved each other. One way or another, as Bill said, we would always be a part of each other's life.

I finished writing the profile of Harry Winston ("The Big Stone"). I wrote a "Letter from Bern" about what was going on in Switzerland and sent it off to Bill. ("...the inhabitants of all the country's twenty-two cantons tell one another the same joke about their President. The joke runs as follows: FIRST SWISS: 'Who's going to be the new President?' SECOND SWISS: 'How would I know? I don't even know who the *old* President is.' The most sedate Swiss is likely to burst into wild laughter at this joke, and there is some pride in the laughter, too, for the people of Switzerland regard the joke as an indication of their success in decentralizing bureaucratic power while maintaining their federal unity"—12/12/53.)

Then I went to London and walked around for hours, thinking about Dickens and Bill. When Bill called, I told him I was going to visit Cambridge. He asked me to walk along the banks of the Cam and up Jesus Lane, where he had lived in Boardinghouse 14. In Cambridge, I decided to skip Jesus Lane. Instead, I went to look at the great King's College Chapel. I thought briefly about God and needing help, but the setting was too grand for me. In a nearby restaurant, I ate roast beef and Yorkshire pudding that made me ill. When I got back to London, in my hotel room, I found a small measure of distraction in making a vow never to eat English roast beef again.

Then I found out that I could get a reservation on the New York–bound *Liberté,* the ship I had taken to Europe three months earlier. When Bill telephoned, I told him I could get the booking. But we found ourselves still floundering about over our course of action. After we had been on the phone for half an hour, he burst out passionately that he didn't care anymore about problems or reasons; he just wanted to look into my face and give me his love. He was putting his existence on the line for me. I felt that I could no longer avoid the responsibility I felt for him. The next day I told him I was definitely planning to take the *Liberté* home. He sent me a telegram saying he would be waiting for me.

On the ship, I spent most of my time walking around and around on the deck. I can't remember anything at all about my return trip except that every time I went to my suitcase for fresh clothes, I had to dig under a sheaf of Bill's telegrams and cables. But at least I returned with a finished manuscript of the Harry Winston profile. I was back in New York just before Christmas. Bill greeted me with a gift—a gold bracelet engraved with our initials and the date of our last day together before I had sailed away the previous September. We both knew that the separation had been a failure. If anything, my months abroad had strengthened our feelings. We agreed that we were overwhelmed by our emotional need to be together. My old assumptions about my life had become irrelevant.

I had to ask myself again what those assumptions about my life really were, and what they meant. In the past, every time that I had thought about Marriage, I had always thought "intolerable." But that was in relation to the young doctor and to others, too. With Bill, I never got that closed-in feeling; it was marriage without the capital "M," and that was more than tolerable.

"I don't give up the fight for you to have everything you need, everything, but I think that for the time being, in spite of all the frightful difficulties, we have to stay together," Bill said. I accepted what he said. It felt right. This time, I wasn't aware of making any kind of fateful "decision." He told me over and over again that I was, in fact, his wife, and that's what it always felt like to me. He was in my life, as I was in his, and both of us moved ahead together. "For the time being" turned out to be forty years.

CHAPTER 6

FIXED IN MEMORY

I now knew that I belonged with Bill no matter what the circumstances, and that I would belong with him all my life. We were collaborators, partners, and friends, both personally and professionally. But was I, after all, that banality of banalities "the other woman"? And if so, what *was* I as "the other woman" anyway?

I certainly never felt like a banality. As a matter of fact, I never felt like "the other woman." Bill would say to me, "You are my wife." He said it; without question that made it so. Together, we were happy. Together, we were true friends and allies, and we both found joy in being alive. In trying to deal with the destructive forces, I now feel, I was ineffective. I may have been pummeled by them myself. Perhaps I might have fought harder against them, but I felt helpless, and I felt fatefully drawn to accepting a particular role in his life.

I began to understand how Bill's feeling of nonexistence—so debilitating in other realms—worked powerfully, "magically," to use that favorite word again, to drive us together. It was as if the emotional tenacity that was absent from so much of his life had found its full center here, in the space we eventually carved out for ourselves. Here, his feelings undercut everything else. Relatives and others attempted to step in and change the situation. We were talked at by people who cared about both of us. No effort to separate us was greater than the effort we made ourselves. All efforts failed.

Other people had glimpses of Bill outside of work—a dinner party here, a funeral service there, most occasions involving his children—but he kept the wall up between himself and others. "Do you know who I am?" he would ask me, when we had made love. He would know the answer. And he would say to me again, "Please do not let me forget my own life."

He confided to me desperate thoughts about himself, but nonetheless he would tell me how lucky we were to be in whatever day or whatever hour or whatever instant we were in together. At every succeeding birthday I had with him, he made me feel that the years were illusory, but our love was real; our love was in what he called a "changeless" place. And so I was able to grow older feeling that I was indeed in a changeless place.

I was in the life with Bill, certainly a full partner in it, in what Bill called "the wonder of everything that happens between you and me." He would say that it was "someone else's life" that he had been living before we started our life together.

Bill spoke honestly to me about his life at home, and, he told me, he continued to speak honestly to his wife about what was happening to him. He still could not act unilaterally and leave his family, and I still would not and could not ask him to. He cared about Cecille. He told me he prayed for Cecille to find a real life for herself. He said he had asked Cecille to leave him, but this she was unable to do. But he could no longer live as he had been living. And, he said, with all this, some of the despair that had encompassed him for so many years was lifting. Our home, he said, was our place of light and promise.

Every time we looked into each other's eyes, we knew that we would always be together as friends.

Along with everybody I admired at the magazine, I was thinking only of how great it was to have him in the job. It never occurred to me to wonder if he wanted it.

I began to feel at peace with myself. I stopped the back-and-forth thinking about my past assumptions. The theoretical formula for my life that I had automatically absorbed from my parents seemed to have become a bit altered, but in the reality of my life, I felt I was living it anyway. It never bothered me that I didn't have a "Mrs." attached to my name. I never thought of myself as a "mistress," a term that to me still carries with it an image of a heavily mascaraed woman in a corny movie, wearing a negligee and sitting around sulking and painting her fingernails. "Our life" is the expression we favored. "Having an affair," that other common expression, didn't seem to fit my life with Bill either. That one, to me, connotes a casual, meaningless romp or a cavalier dalliance.

Years later, when Jacqueline Kennedy Onassis and Maurice Tempelsman revealed publicly that they were making their life together—identifying what he was to her as "companion"—even though he was married to another woman, Bill and I agreed that the word "companion" was inadequate to describe our own relationship. We were glad that William Buckley, who occasionally seemed to feel called upon to make some severe pronouncements on "adultery," didn't make any regarding Onassis and Tempelsman, and we were also glad that no one seemed to care to make any about us. Most people in our office responded respectfully to us and didn't intrude in any way. Bill never put on any disguises, nor did I. Out in the open, we were respectful of ourselves. Bill would be at ease, in charge, natural, normal. Neither one of us was ever embarrassed. Recently, an anonymous spectator was quoted in a gossip column as saying that he once saw Bill "blushing beet red" with me. Inaccurate. Bill was incapable of engendering a cliché, in deed as well as in word.

Although I was more shielded from hurt than Bill or his wife in our unconventional situation, I was hardly unaware of the hurt hammering the other two. "All decent people feel guilt," a Hungarian psychoanalyst once said. And Bill, the most decent as well as the most reasonable of men, seemed beyond help in his overwhelming guilt and pain. Bill and I shielded each other simply by never knowingly doing anything hurtful one to the other. "We must hold each other close, as if there were no circumstances but only the single circumstance that we love each other and belong together," he would say. He brought me into his life completely. Every time I tried to sort out what I would have to give up in my life with Bill, the list became shorter. I could even have a child with him. Finally, there seemed to be only one item on the list: a marriage certificate. The list of compensations, meanwhile, was extraordinary.

The purity of Bill's literary taste seemed to me to be total. Romantically, his taste never was at odds with that purity. He revered St. Valentine's Day, for instance, although he didn't care much for real holidays, and he sought out Valentines for me that were genuine antiques, replete with white lace and golden thread. I have a stack of them—with scores of hearts bedecked with chubby-cheeked and sailor-suited children and pink-and-white angels and bearing "Think of me" declarations, as well as poems he would never have published in his magazine.

As in any ceremonial joining, we made sacred pledges to each other about the exclusivity of our bodies and of our spirits. From that point on, I never had a single regret about my decision—not then, and to this day, not now. Strangely, when I was away from Bill, I didn't pine for him. I often enjoyed being alone, because aloneness had been my habit. Yet every time we met after being apart I felt surprise at how happy I was to see him again. This never changed. Then there was an actual moment when I began to feel powerfully that I belonged with this man, no matter what the circumstances, and that I would belong with him all my life. Every time we looked into each other's eyes, we knew that we would always be together as friends.

With Cecille's knowledge, Bill installed a private telephone in his bedroom, with a number he gave solely to me. We could reach each other at any hour. We began and ended our waking hours on the telephone with each other. In the middle of the night we sometimes telephoned each other and fell asleep talking. Our lives were joined. My running-away days were over.

We found a two-room apartment—in a hotel ten blocks south of Bill and Cecille's. It was one that nobody else wanted, because the bedroom—the fine view of Central Park notwithstanding—had been converted entirely into a gigantic closet to hold the clothes of the previous occupant, Marlene Dietrich. The place was on the fifteenth floor, but Bill had no problem with the elevator, no problem with claustrophobia. We had a kitchenette and used it for daily lunches and some suppers. In 1958 we found the twelfth-floor apartment in the newly built house in the neighborhood, and we started buying furniture.

Summers remained difficult for Bill. He hated to go out of New York City. He and Cecille continued to rent a furnished house in Bronxville, and he continued to resist going there. In one house, he said, "there aren't even any books." He still had a local fireman drive him into the city every day, and, as usual, he would pick me up on the way to work, and we would go to the office together. The fireman would drive his car back to Bronxville without him. After supper, Bill usually hired a Carey car to drive him back to Bronxville. He wouldn't want to go back alone and would ask me to accompany him, which I did, thus giving us forty-five additional minutes together. Then I would go back to the city alone.

We couldn't get enough of each other. In the mornings, we used to stop and have breakfast at a neat little place in Rockefeller Center that served freshly squeezed orange juice. For lunch, we went to our apartment, where I always made the same lunch: scrambled eggs, William Greenberg's freshly baked minirolls with sweet butter, sugar cookies, coffee.

We would leave *The New Yorker* together nightly. We never experienced even a moment of "conflict of interest" problems, for the simple reason that we never had any conflict of interest. I had too much pride in my work ever to ask for any special favors. If I wanted to see Bill in his office, I called his secretary, like everyone else, and asked if he could see me. I never doubted that as my editor, Bill accepted and published my writing on its merits. Each of us, as editor and writer, had a self-confidence that was total.

If anything, Bill would bend over backward not to favor me in any way. Once I wrote a parody of a par-for-the-course book review by a pompous, pretentious, cliché-prone "literary" critic. The piece was about a new book called *How to Play Tennis the Professional Way;* its title was "The Centrality of the Net," and the subtitle was "A powerful, definitive and intensely moral account of tennis in a 20th-century context." Bill thought the piece was funny and wanted to publish it, but his editor in charge of book reviews disagreed. So the piece was rejected. (It was published in the *New York Herald Tribune*'s book review section and, to my satisfaction, made a big hit with people on the summer beaches.)

From the *New Yorker* office, we would head uptown in a taxi and stop for supper. It was a high-cholesterol routine, and we grew fond of it: home-cooked food at the restaurant then run by the New York Exchange for Women's Work, or our favorite French cuisine at La Caravelle. But the routine had its healthy aspects. Bill disliked the odor of cigarettes. I immediately gave up smoking. He was afraid of "drinking." I gave up martinis. He also didn't like speeding. With him, I drove at thirty-five miles per hour; alone, I was a speeder. On weekends, we would take our own kind of "vacation," hiding out from the world at the Plaza or at the Carlyle and calling room

"I write for *you*," his writers would say to him. They all said the same words: "I write for *you*." He would look embarrassed when they said it to him.

service. Today there are doormen, elevator operators, and waiters still at the latter hotel who remember us fondly and with good will.

Bill assured me that Cecille was going along with our arrangements. From time to time, I would think: Maybe she loves him so much she wants him to have what keeps him alive. Then, on many mornings, when he picked me up, I would see the familiar misery in his face. Bill never became inured to his guilt, but he never gave even the slightest intimation of wanting to change our own life.

I never asked him any questions about his past life with Cecille. Whatever he told me—about his marriage, about his illness on the ship in 1929, about Cecille in his early days at *The New Yorker,* about his dislike of Bronxville life, and so forth—he told me of his own volition. I accepted his views of all of it.

"We must arrest our love in midflight," Bill once said. "And we fix it forever as it is today, a point of pure light that will reach into eternity."

I may not have understood the full power of his need when I made my commitment to him, but I knew it soon.

We never became targets of public gossip. We did not need to be with anyone else, but if we found ourselves with others, we felt at ease with them. Our very efforts to lead our life outside of his marriage drove us to make more and more powerful connections with each other.

Cecille became a party to our actions. Bill was truthful and open with her at all times. He told her no lies. Lying was among the things he never knew how to do. Bill agonized over the situation but faced it alone, although he was able to talk about it to me. He felt no need for secrecy. It was almost as though the facts of his marriage all had their rightful place. For years before he ever met me, he explained, he had

Our life together continued self-contained, in a corridor of freedom we managed to build for ourselves.

faced and dealt with other maelstroms, and just as I was completely outside of those in the past, I was not part of this one, either. I felt I was truly outside of it. It became, for the most part, an abstraction. But that didn't diminish the sorrow.

Bill loved his children, and when he talked about them to me, they were not an abstraction; in fact, I absorbed his special sense of them completely. He told me everything about his children throughout our years together. The children were real. But Bill and I had to live, he said repeatedly, as if there were only the single circumstance that we loved each other and belonged together. He was able to make it seem so, and I found that he made it possible for me to go along with him. "Our love has a life of its own," he would say. For me, this was what became the norm. I would try to think about Cecille, to imagine what life was for her. But I would find myself unable to give her reality.

After forty years, our love-making had the same passion, the same energies (alarming to me, at first, in our early weeks together), the same tenderness, the same inventiveness, the same humor, the same textures as it had in the beginning. It never deteriorated, our later wrinkles, blotches, and scars of age notwithstanding. We never changed. Things that were supposed to happen to a couple after ten years, or after twenty years, or after forty years never happened to us. Our love never became stale. It never became confrontational. It never became bitter. We were never enveloped in frustrations. We never drifted into deceptions. Our friendship with each other grew and flourished over the years. Why should it have been any different? Once we made our final commitment to each other, there was no basis for any kind of conflict between us. He never reproached me, not once in our years together. He never criticized me, not once. If I questioned him about a seemingly outlandish action of his, a sentiment, an opinion, his answers always made some kind of sense to me. I accepted his answers; I accepted him. We were able to nurture our friendship consistently with openness, honesty, and reality. With each other, we had no secrets. And I felt no guilt in our sexual and emotional closeness.

His understanding of and sympathy for femininity were noticed by many people, but he didn't often, with others, reveal his very powerful masculinity. I thoroughly enjoyed this side of him. Bill liked to be free to act sexist at times, and I got a sort of kick out of his sexist posturings. Bill consistently made me feel feminine, attractive, desirable, appreciated, interesting, and secure. For almost half a century, we were able to resist conventional rules and hold to our own. And Bill was able to give me the kind of unmitigated and privileged happiness that survives death itself.

How did he hold on to life? "Who am I?" he would ask me. "Am I really here?" he would ask. Why was I able to join my life with his? I respected the facts he told me about himself in exactly the way I have always respected facts given to me by everybody I have written about as a reporter. I would discover that "I am there but not there" was, to him, a fact. And it was deeply tied to another fact about him: Unlike most of us, who push away the feeling of death until the end, that feeling was in him always, and might be dispelled, he said, only by "a miracle."

Eventually, in my life with Bill Shawn, I felt no deprivation, no frustration, no absences, no holes, no misshapeness, no unanswered needs. That was the miracle. For the most part, there was nothing baroque in our life and nothing feverish. He suffered pain and sorrow because of what was happening to Cecille. He did not conceal that suffering from me. But he made a single, unqualified fact plain; he said he was unable to change his course with me. With time, as our life went on in an atmosphere of serenity and love, I began to understand what he meant by "I am there but not there." "Our feelings have the final say" was not a matter of his saying it and my blindly following along. Now his feelings were mine too. Comfort and serenity and quiet were mine day after day and night after night; they were becoming fixed already in my memory. Nothing and nobody could cancel them out.

I found myself developing extraordinary patience and extraordinary sympathy for Bill's revelations about himself. In the office, if he suffered a paper cut on a finger and saw blood, he would come into my office, looking pale and embarrassed, and sit down for a few minutes. Then the color would return to his face, and without saying anything, he would leave.

I learned not to dismiss his fears. Most of the time, even the uncomplicated, practical, ordinary accommodations to living baffled him. When he got into a taxicab, for example, he would sit lopsided, in the most uncomfortable position possible. If I suggested that he move his body to a more upright, sensible position, he seemed to feel he might be disturbing or bothering the taxi driver. If I suggested to him that he would not hurt anybody, and, in fact, he might take positive action for himself *and* for the driver by sitting comfortably, his lovely face would break up into suppressed laughter, understanding laughter, at himself. But he could not bring himself to move to a more comfortable position. "I do not know how to do it," he would say.

His tipping habits continued to be outlandish. In restaurants, he would tip fifty percent of the price of the dinner. One balmy evening after dinner, Bill, my son, Erik, and I were walking up Fifth Avenue and passed a street musician, a saxophonist, who was playing Gershwin. Bill took out his wallet, peeled off the top bill, and placed it in the man's open music case. I saw that it was a hundred-dollar bill.

"Why?" I asked.

Bill looked embarrassed. "Gershwin," he said, barely able to get the name out.

Bill equated violence of any kind, even a violent thought, with death, and he was incapable of acting with violence toward anybody, even when he was angry.

The longest argument I can remember stemmed from some skeptical remarks I had made about President John Kennedy's press secretary, Pierre Salinger. To Bill, Kennedy was a hero, not to be put down in any way. Pierre Salinger was, as I saw it, trying to promote a certain image of John and Jackie Kennedy, and although I admired them, I was also critical and had many reservations. They were not, I said, what they pretended to be. I felt that Pierre Salinger, on television, was deliberately and carefully trying to manipulate *me* into a kind of uncritical emotion beyond admiration. It was the only time Bill made me feel not only that my skepticism was unwarranted but that I was being cynical and unfair. So my feelings were hurt, and I told Bill that I thought he was being naive. Our only other argument concerned the original Broadway musical *West Side Story*. Bill was strongly impressed by Leonard Bernstein's music, but I criticized the book's depiction of the mainly Puerto Rican characters. I grew more and more frustrated as I argued that the characters were false, and therefore the music and lyrics merely intensified the falseness. For some reason, neither one of us retreated from that argument for hours after we had left the theatre and gone home. Two genuine arguments over a period of forty years.

Bill's recourse, if I seemed not to be listening to his reasoning, was to pound his Briggs umbrella (which he carried daily, rain or no rain) on the sidewalk, breaking it. The breakage would have an instant effect: Both of us would fall into a paroxysm of laughter, and we would not feel like arguing any more. And we would go as soon as possible to Brooks Brothers and buy a new Briggs. Physical violence to others—real or fictional—that brought injury or harm was another matter.

For some reason, sitting at our piano one day, Bill suddenly started improvising, jazz I had never before heard him play. Then he said, turning to me with a small, unbelieving smile, that he was beginning to feel free, to have some hope. And I was part of it. That was joy to hear and joy to feel.

CHAPTER 7

PARTNERS

Bill loved jazz, and he loved to play it. He loved the songs of George Gershwin and Cole Porter and Harold Arlen and Yip Harburg. He loved songs like "Last Night When We Were Young" and "Our Love Is Here to Stay" and "They Can't Take That Away from Me." He reveled in listening to Louis Armstrong playing and singing, with Velma Middleton, W. C. Handy's "St. Louis Blues." He wept joyously over the piano playing of ninety-year-old Eubie Blake. I was happy hanging out with him, going to small clubs or bars to hear Mabel Mercer or Blossom Dearie or Rosemary Clooney or Joe Williams. We were regulars at Birdland and at the Half Note and at the Blue Angel and at the Village Vanguard. He was overcome with excitement to hear Thelonius Monk. We went to the Hickory House to hear Stan Getz, and we went to the Cookery to hear Alberta Hunter. He would laugh out loud if he caught Dizzy Gillespie playing and singing "Salt Peanuts." He liked to say that his birth date (August 31) was pretty close to Charlie Parker's (August 29) and Lester Young's (August 27), and he would make a special effort to get to hear one or both of them near the end of that month. And once in a while, at the Embers, for example, he would be surprised and thrilled to stumble upon Coleman Hawkins and Roy Eldridge playing with each other and with Marian McPartland. As time went on, he loved to listen to the Beatles and to Paul Simon and to James Taylor and to Sting. But most of all, as I've said, Bill loved Duke Ellington. As soon as he started earning some money he became a regular at the Cotton Club, he told me, just to see and hear Duke Ellington. Later on, we would go to see and hear him in concerts, in clubs, in churches. Bill loved what Duke Ellington composed and the way Duke Ellington played and talked and dressed and sat at the piano.

Bill seemed to become more and more eager to feel carefree and lighthearted. We would go to the ballet, and afterward, out on the street, handing me his umbrella, he would show me how to do an entrechat. We would be among the first to attend new movies (we kept going back to see *The Umbrellas of Cherbourg* and *Wild Strawberries* because they had a special hold on Bill), especially English movies, particularly ones about the English working class. (We went to see Mike Leigh's *High Hopes* three times during its first week's run.) We formed friendships with a few other couples, not writers, who liked jazz, and we would go to dinner with them and hunt down performers—the jazz pianist Joey Bushkin, for example. Bill was able to relax with friends such as Lola and Nathan Finkelstein, who were in the beauty-parlor business; and young John Schreiber, a music-and-entertainment impresario whose jazz expertise and knowledgeability rivaled Bill's; and Cathy Register and her husband, John, an extraordinary painter. Bill would be gallant and funny and outgoing with them. He composed many songs, among others: "Empty Town," "Something up My Sleeve," "Save It, Pretty Poppa, Save It for Me," and "Thank You for Being the Girl You Are" (he thanked me in the song for "letting" him fall in love with me). We had the last song copyrighted, and because he never wanted to put his name on anything, we had the words and music copyrighted under a name Bill made up: David Hope.

There were contradictions in Bill. He wore conservative clothes but yearned to dress like Fred Astaire. We went to an expensive men's shop on Park Avenue and bought him some Fred Astaire–type clothes, including an elegant silver-colored silk sports jacket, yellow silk pants, and some yellow swimming trunks. We splurged on some Pratesi towels because Bill said he longed to feel the soft terry cloth on his face. He revealed, without apology, that he yearned for a taste, just a taste, of some of the luxury items that were so often advertised in his magazine. He enjoyed samplings of beauty, he said. When we began looking for items for our apartment, he introduced me to names I hadn't known—Scalamandré, Porthault, Knoll, Baccarat. We didn't go crazy; we sampled modestly.

We bought a TR-3 sports car, in British racing green, and we bought a sporty black-and-white-checked cap for Bill to wear while driving it. The day we picked up the car we drove over the Manhattan Bridge in the Triumph, with Bill at the wheel, and went to Brooklyn for a festive steak dinner at the famous old Gage and Tollner's restaurant. The very next day, we got into the Triumph, drove up to the Grossinger's resort in the Catskills, registered in a room, and went swimming in the pool, Bill in his yellow trunks. I was aware of Bill's fears and phobias, his claustrophobia, his inability to "travel," but we simply got into the Triumph and took off without discussion of any phobias or fears. It was truly a "miracle." He loved driving the Triumph. He'd get behind the wheel, take off his hat, put on his checked cap, and off we'd go. We took corny "on vacation" snapshots of each other à la Esther Williams and Fred Astaire in resort clothes. Once we drove out to East Hampton and walked on the beach, holding hands as we watched the ocean. Another time, in the winter, we drove to Grossinger's and went ice-skating and skiing. (Bill hated

We bought a TR-3 sports car, in British racing green, and we bought a sporty black-and-white cap for Bill to wear while driving it.

He'd get behind the wheel, take off his hat, put on his checked cap, and off we'd go.

snow. He hated the cold. But he went ice-skating at Grossinger's with a kind of glee.) Once, we managed to get to Boston and stayed at the Ritz-Carlton; we feasted on crab cakes in the dining room and strolled in the Public Garden.

I began to notice a change in Bill's face. I started taking photographs of his face, rejoicing in what I now saw in it—the lightness, the sensuality. His moments of joy became so deeply affecting to me that I found myself happy just to see the happiness in him. These moments came in bed, of course, as expected, but they also came at unexpected times. When, for example, we saw Zero Mostel in *A Funny Thing Happened on the Way to the Forum,* we laughed not only throughout the show but hours and days afterward; something we might see on the street, or a word from a waiter in a restaurant, would remind us of Zero and would set us off into sieges of near-hysteria.

We began to have more fun with the way Bill dressed. After we bought the Fred Astaire clothes, it became sort of a mission of mine to see a new hat on his head. He liked a certain kind of felt hat with a small brim. Lola Finkelstein told me about Borsalino hats, so she brought one from Italy, and he wore it. On weekends, Bill took to wearing a plaid sports cap. Then we visited J. Press and he got fitted for a couple of new suits, similar to his old blue suit, but in cashmere. When we went for the final fittings, he tried on the suits with childlike, self-conscious pleasure, wondering aloud how such trivial self-indulgence could make him feel so much more lighthearted. He told me that putting on a new suit made him feel happier, and although that didn't make any "sense," he liked it. Bill took a great interest in my clothes, and from him I acquired taste and judgment about all of it, including the purity of colors.

One semester, at Columbia University, we audited a course given by Meyer Schapiro on the Impressionist painters. We made exciting discoveries together—Lenny Bruce, Mike

Nichols and Elaine May, Richard Pryor, Woody Allen. Bill marveled at them and tried to figure out whether all of them might write for *The New Yorker.* We walked, arm in arm, all over the city. One afternoon when Bill was wearing his sporty cap a street photographer snapped our picture while we were walking. I happened to look at my watch. Four o'clock. Bill's "hour of hope." At that moment, Bill heard a man say: "You ain't gonna get nothin' but outta a job—thas all." Bill wrote down the words on the envelope containing our photograph. It became "our saying." Over the years, one of us would say it to the other often, very often, at appropriate times.

Food was one thing Bill did not have any phobias about. Much has been made of the myth that he would eat only cornflakes. Actually, he loved to eat great food. He favored some wonderful classic restaurants, and there he would eat ample meals, with vanilla or raspberry soufflé for dessert. He enjoyed introducing me to restaurants he said he had always wanted to frequent. I accompanied him to Henri Soule's Le Pavillon, and both of us became addicted to food on that level. Later on, we switched to the Pavillon-offspring restaurant La Caravelle, which became our regular restaurant for the next twenty-five years.

The depression Bill said he had suffered from for years was ebbing, but he was philosophical about its comings and goings. He accepted it, as he did his claustrophobia and agoraphobia, which were also subsiding. Up and down in the elevators—fine. Trips to the countryside—fine. Sitting in a crowded theatre—fine.

Bill was attracted physically to all kinds of women. He lusted for beautiful models pictured in magazines; for wild American movie stars, such as Louise Brooks; for French movie stars, such as Simone Signoret or Annie Girardot or Françoise Rosay or Jeanne Moreau; for English movie stars, such as Julie Christie; for Italian movie stars, such as Anna Magnani or Sophia Loren; for Swedish movie stars, such as

And, on the highway, he wouldn't even think about having an exit nearby.

Bill never put on any disguises, nor did I. Out in the open, we were natural and respectful of ourselves.

He wanted something more for himself. Not much. A small taste of something.

We drove in our Triumph to baseball games and to race-tracks.

We got into the Triumph, drove up to the Grossinger's resort in the Catskills, registered, and went swimming in the pool, Bill in his yellow trunks.

Liv Ullmann or Bibi Andersson; for big brains, such as Susan Sontag or Hannah Arendt; for singers who phrased like Mabel Mercer or Rosemary Clooney; for women with little-girl looks; for women with Alice-in-Wonderland hair or gamin haircuts; for strange women he had noticed for an instant, days or months or years earlier, getting into a taxi or buying a newspaper; for fat women (the fatter the better); for elderly women who resembled his mother (full-bosomed); for athletic women, as long as they looked and moved like the tennis star Evonne Goolagong; for women wearing aprons or silk-print dresses or sleek suits or nothing. In later years, he was attracted to Whoopi Goldberg, Vanessa Redgrave, and Madonna. After I did the story for *The New Yorker* about the Miss America contest (following Miss New York State through the competition from start to finish), he watched the contestants, when they started appearing on television, every September for the rest of his life, annually bestowing his affection on his own choice for winner. He loved women in general, and he loved the thought of women. He was drawn to Jacqueline Kennedy, and he worried about her. Whenever he saw a well-known woman in a well-known job, whether it was Gro Harlem Brundtland, the prime minister of Norway, or Barbara Walters of television, he always looked at, and saw, the woman behind the job. For the most part, he thought, women were more interesting than men.

The more feminine a woman was, the more interesting she was to Bill. He enjoyed the role of protecting the woman, of having the woman dependent on him, of feeling stronger than the woman, of being the gentleman down to the marrow. He was probably the last man in town to remove his hat in an elevator when a woman entered (no matter how many packages, in addition to his briefcase and umbrella, he held in his arms). He was a big hat-lifter in general. He would lift his hat to a passing baby in a pram. For me, the equation was fine, and I enjoyed it.

He would have affecting experiences—he called them "bizarre" experiences—with "memories" of women—Anna Magnani, for example. I enjoyed hearing about them. Somehow or other, he was pushing away the confining walls around him. I rejoiced in all of it for him and with him. I wanted so much for him to be free.

Among the myriad pressures brought to bear on us was a parade of psychoanalysts. Before I was on the scene, the first psychoanalyst Bill went to was Dr. Ruth Hankendi, a Hungarian woman, who was, much to Bill's surprise, very appealing. She had her office in her home. What he liked most of all in going to her, he told me, was the wonderful smell of cooking in her home. He yearned for the cooking, but he had to settle for the odors. He told her about his depression, about feeling he had taken wrong turns in his life. Nevertheless, the aroma of her cooking cheered him up. She was very sympathetic toward Bill, he told me, but she was at a loss to offer him anything except sympathy. A few years later, she became ill and died.

The next psychoanalyst, Dr. Franz S. Cohn, an elderly Austrian, turned out to offer even more than cooking odors for Bill's comfort. By then I was in the picture, and Bill seemed to be getting encouragement from Dr. Cohn in his feelings about me. I would meet Bill every time he emerged, happy and excited, from a session with Dr. Cohn. "I love talking with him," Bill said. "He has brilliant ideas." He eagerly read passages to me from Dr. Cohn's writings in *The Psychoanalytic Quarterly*. For example: "The poet, like the hypochondriac, experiences loneliness, regression, and depersonalization. He knows, however, how to protect his morbidity, and his salvation is that he can speak to the world and himself with the soothing voice of the mother." This was Bill's kind of stuff. And more: "Sexual libido helps to form external relationships but individual man, like the poet Goncourt, also has to find an odd companionship with himself, and even in this relationship he will be haunted by sensations which we have learned to recognize as Time. The solution depends on the strength of the narcissism. If the access to these sources is blocked, we may find a condition of loneliness, boredom, or hypochondriasis." Bill was especially taken with the following: "Saintly people have submitted to a life of the dead, renouncing all possessions, and thus surrendering to a lifetime transfiguration. Their present must have seemed irrelevant to them, an existence suspended in time. We ordinary people of our time imagine ourselves to be well protected against such a philosophy."

Bill somehow felt support from Dr. Cohn in the course he had chosen for his life. Soon, however, pressure was placed on Bill when another family doctor intruded professionally into the situation, disagreeing with Dr. Cohn. Bill, naturally, started worrying, not about himself, but about Dr. Cohn's facing some kind of trouble in his profession. So, very reluctantly, Bill gave in and left him.

From then on, a string of psychoanalysts was enlisted in pursuit of Bill, including one who kept losing her notes about him and kept forgetting his name, and another one who had written a book about Jonathan Swift and wanted to write one about Bill. (Bill declined.) Bill would tell me that going to these psychoanalysts took some burden off him, because it served a purpose: it kept a focus on his "neuroses" as the cause of his actions, instead of a focus on his life.

At one point, I, too, let myself be persuaded to go to a psychoanalyst recommended by the devotee of Jonathan Swift. My analyst turned out to be a charming, sophisticated, and wise Hungarian (he had studied with Sándor Ferenczi) who told me he had read and enjoyed *Vertical and Horizontal.* He spent a lot of time sharing with me his own storehouse of wonderful jokes about other psychoanalysts. He had also read *Picture,* and we talked a lot about reporting and writing. I went to him for a few months, and then he advised me not to go in for analysis. "Remember," he said before I left him, "all decent people feel guilt."

CHAPTER 8

EDITOR-IN-CHIEF

Over the years, all the turmoil in Bill's personal life hardly surfaced in the office of *The New Yorker.* Both of us kept it where it belonged. As I have said, our colleagues gradually came to know about our relationship. They ran into us together in restaurants, on weekend walks on the streets in the city, at movies, at concerts, at the theatre. Old friends of Bill's and Cecille's continued their friendships with them. Bill's sons, Wallace and Allen, came to hear about us from other people, but in accord with Cecille's wishes, Wallace and Allen had no discussion with their parents about us. Their love of and loyalty to their mother guided them in their actions. They asked no questions of their father. He was there for them when they wanted him. Both sons, as they grew into adulthood, would have long one-on-one private lunches with Bill, often at the Algonquin or at the Plaza, to talk about themselves.

Miraculously, Bill was able to carry on in his creative relationships with the scores of his particular writers and artists, with his editors in the art and fiction departments, and with his nonfiction editors, who helped on pieces. He relied on sensitive, generous, devoted, and talented editors, all of whom have become legendary and beloved in their own right—William Maxwell, John Bennet, Gardner Botsford, Charles Patrick Crow, William Knapp, Susan Moritz, Veronica Geng, Robert MacMillan, Robert Gerdy and Robert Bingham—and even before them Hobart G. Weekes and Rogers E. M. Whitaker. He relied on the editorial experts, each one unique and superbly informed—Eleanor Gould and Ann Goldstein in overall final editing for grammar, logic, and clarity; Roger Angell, Charles McGrath, Gwyneth Cravens, Linda Asher, Robert Henderson, Frances Kiernan, Daniel Menaker, and Mary Kirstead in fiction; Howard Moss in poetry; Martin Baron and Peter Canby in checking, with their host of experts; Christopher Shay in the library; Anne Hall, Peter DeVries (also a writer), and Lee Lorenz in art; Patrick Keogh in makeup—most of them trained in the tradition of unobtrusive but irreplaceable people such as James Geraghty and Carmine Peppe, whose names are little known. Some of the editors, like William Maxwell and Roger Angell, have been outstanding writers as well. Gardner Botsford, one of the quietest among the unpublicized and unheralded, is one of the most stylish and original writers of all.

Bill himself stood, with what everyone around him recognized as his inventiveness and ingenuity, his humanity and wisdom, as the supportive figure holding it all up. For the writer, he was, as I wrote in my part of *The New Yorker* tribute to him after his death, "your best reader, wonderfully responsive, providing the instant corroboration you needed." To the writers, every one of us, he gave the freedom to find ourselves and be ourselves. And yet, as my years with him went on, he couldn't find that freedom for himself in his own work. Our life together continued, self-contained, in a corridor of freedom we managed to build for ourselves. Outside of that, Bill gave himself always to what was, in his view, "best for the magazine."

Bill carried on with all his duties and responsibilities to the publisher—Raoul Fleischmann at first and eventually his son, Peter Fleischmann—and there never was a break in the interminable meetings and conferences he held about the life and survival of *The New Yorker.* Among other things, he continually helped the business department in their efforts to sell the magazine by demonstrating to them, clearly, what it was they were trying to sell. Throughout all of this, he never gave a sign of being a "ghost," of "not existing," of his agony, or of his guilt. For everybody at *The New Yorker,* he felt he had to be the strong one, the infallible one, the one they knew they could count on, in short, perfect.

In the fall of 1976, when he had been editor-in-chief for a quarter of a century, he spelled out his passionate views about the uniqueness of the magazine and of what he called its "friendly, gentle, free, informal, democratic atmosphere." He also described—and actually diagrammed—the way this atmosphere was produced, the way it worked, and the way he was controlling all of it. The occasion for this revelation was a notice from the Newspaper Guild that "some members of the salaried, job-holding staff had asked the Guild to organize the editorial employees of *The New Yorker.*" Bill was profoundly hurt and upset by this news. When he showed me the notice, he was shaken and disheartened. Until then, I hadn't heard anything about it, but when Bill told me the names of some of the staff members who wanted a union, I was surprised; several of them were my friends, and the rest were the hard workers who helped the well-paid "names" enjoy their labors. Why should they want a union? It was puzzling, but given my congenital proclivity to be on the side of the workers, I was immediately sympathetic to them. I told that to Bill, who, as usual, did not take offense at my point of view. I said that there had to be some *reason,* some break in his communication with the staff, to have brought on the situation. I felt that there *had* been such a break. Almost immediately it turned out that the major complaints and grievances—about salaries and promotions—had never been brought to Bill's attention; they had stopped with some of his aides, who had taken it upon themselves to "protect" Bill, to keep him from being "bothered."

So Bill wrote, in his characteristic, lucid prose, a letter to the staff, saying he was not opposed to unions in principle, but that he thought that a union would be "harmful to our staff, and therefore to the magazine."

He said that if he thought a union would truly improve the lot of the staff, he would be for it. For thirty-eight years, he explained, as managing editor and editor, he had fought steadily for higher salaries, and for higher payments for the published material, and also for instituting a retirement plan and a profit-sharing plan. But, he went on: "*The New Yorker* is a creative, collaborative enterprise unlike any other. It is in many ways unique among publications. . . . I think that a union might introduce a rigidity in the way the office functions, hinder the free flow of people from one kind of work to another, reduce the opportunity for experiment, and reduce the emphasis on the individual. . . . What we have here—and that goes for all of us—is freedom; and I don't want to see us give it up in any way."

Over the following month, Bill, while going on no less intensively with his regular work and with our life, talked for hours to the people who had asked for the union. Then he wrote another letter to the staff, a much longer letter than the previous one, in which he patiently set out to explain "just how our office works." He spoke of the "very odd arrangement" whereby the publisher not only stayed completely out of editorial matters but also never turned down anything the editor wanted regarding salaries and payments. "The decisions, good or bad, were mine," Bill wrote.

The Guild did not come to *The New Yorker.* Without fear of reprisals, all of the organizing committee members in the office went on with their jobs. Certain financial inequities were straightened out. Thereafter, if any staff member had a complaint, he knew exactly where to go with it. The only staff member in the office who continued to grieve over what had happened was Bill Shawn.

Bill once explained some of *The New Yorker*'s changing patterns to Peter Fleischmann, who had become president and publisher of the magazine following the death, in 1969, of his father, Raoul Fleischmann, founder, with Harold Ross, of the magazine. By 1939, when Bill became managing editor, he wrote, "with Ross's generous and open-minded encouragement, I was allowed to give the magazine several new dimensions—intellectual, moral, spiritual—broaden its journalistic scope, add substance and depth to the magazine; in short, help create it." (He was "allowed" to give the magazine new dimensions! That was as far as he ever went in recognizing his achievements. Harold Ross at that point had gone through sixteen previous managing editors.) Bill described how he found the journalistic side of the magazine in a state of disarray, with a tiny staff, and how he started building a staff that would give him the required material. He explained that he took a personal interest in each writer, forming relationships that would make all of them feel secure and enable them to do their best work. He took responsibility, he said, "for their work and for their lives."

Bill never turned away from what he felt was his responsibility to explain, to outline, to state clearly what he believed *The New Yorker* lived by. Occasionally, on a Saturday afternoon, I would sit next to him on our sofa while he patiently wrote—in pen, on a legal pad, supported by one of his Mediterranean Shop writing boards covered with "forget-me-not" paper—in his small, neat, longhand, line after interminable line about what he called "our principles." On the following Monday, he would bring his pages to the office and give them to Mary Painter, his secretary, for typing. I might have preferred to see Bill at his piano on a Saturday, but I enjoyed looking at him, looking at his handwriting, while he explained his "principles."

It was World War II that really changed the magazine, Bill wrote for the advertising people of *The New Yorker* in 1979. "It's been a gradual thing and effected by many people," he said. "It did become more responsible, more aware of what's going on in the world, and more knowledgeable, more thorough, more concerned, and yet trying to cling as hard as possible to humor and to the lightness with which we began, because that element in *The New Yorker* is in its own way just as serious as the most serious things that we publish. Humor is a part of our life here, and without it we would just be an earnest, well-meaning, and probably tedious, magazine. And its humor, I think, is an indispensable element in the magazine and one that is very dear to the people who run the magazine, editorially."

The people working in the advertising department often invited Bill Shawn to come downstairs to their floor and talk to them about *The New Yorker.* When he accepted an invitation and actually appeared down there, they listened in fascination to what he told them.

"They're so touching in their eagerness to learn," Bill would tell me. "Their questions are so intelligent, and they come up to me afterwards, one by one, to thank me. They say they're so grateful to learn about what *The New Yorker* is. They're all such nice people." Once his remarks so strongly affected the business people that they printed them and gave them to advertisers.

"*The New Yorker* is constantly changing," he wrote at one point.

> It has grown deeper, I think. It has also broadened its intellectual range, and even, I'd say, its emotional range. In our early days, in a perfectly sound reaction against the sentimentality

> of much of the writing that was then appearing in American magazines, we went so far in the opposite direction that at times we were afraid of emotion itself. That led to a lot of wonderful wit and humor, but it also sometimes stood in the way of true sentiment or feeling. Today we were less likely to shy away from emotion. At the same time, we were less likely to shy away from ideas. We used to be enamored of facts but a little embarrassed in the presence of ideas—as if all ideas, rather than just some, were pretentious and rather suspect. We no longer feel that way. We've come to respect and enjoy ideas as well as facts.
>
> There is no question that the magazine has come to have a greater social and political and moral awareness, and to feel a greater responsibility. We are not as aloof as we once were.... [We get out] the magazine we have wanted to get out, pursuing our own tastes and interests and disregarding what might be popular or fashionable or commercially promising.... we've never written down or edited down to anyone.... And through it all we've considered humor indispensable, and we've searched for it, clung to it, and nourished it as if our life depended on it—and I think it did.

People from other magazines, along with people who wanted to start new magazines, came to Bill for advice and help. Jann Wenner, then a young man, came to see him when he was trying to get going with *Rolling Stone.*

"You know what he said to me?" Bill reported, looking stunned. "He said, 'I want to pick your brains.' I never heard *that* expression before."

Another time, and again for the business people, Bill wrote:

> These are turbulent times in the magazine world. In the past few years, many old magazines have withered or vanished; new magazines have sprung up; several magazines have transformed their look, or even their character, overnight; to compete with television, and with each other, some of the

mass-circulation magazines have sought larger and larger circulations at almost any cost; a number have offered radical, if not frantic, cuts in what they call their subscription rates; some have spent millions upon millions of dollars on circulation and advertising promotion, with the result that circulations and advertising income have indeed been going up but profits have been going down; many magazines have stopped thinking about themselves as publications designed to enlighten and entertain readers and have begun to think of themselves as advertising mediums; others, the pseudo magazines, instead of following some natural editorial bent, have adopted an editorial "formula" expressly devised to attract and frame advertising; some magazines have devoted more attention to "projecting an image" of what they want to appear to be than they have to considering what they really are; others, instead of contributing whatever they themselves might contribute to the cultural life of the country, have been exploiting what is termed the culture boom (among those that, with opportunistic agility, can and do raise or lower their brows at will, unaware of the fact that the ring is equally false whether you talk down to your readers or live beyond your intellectual means); still others have been riding other booms. In the magazine field, as in so many other fields today, the lines have become blurred—lines between the real thing and the bogus, between the spontaneous and the calculated, between substance and razzle-dazzle, between something that is done because it is worth doing and something that is done because it will sell.

There is nothing we would rather do than enlighten and entertain our readers. On the other hand, *The New Yorker* does not try to guess what its readers want, and does not try—by means of reader surveys, pre-testing, or other highly organized pulse-taking—to find out what they want. In the realm of literature, of art, of creative journalism, to attempt to give readers what they "want" is, circularly, to give them what they already know about and have already had, and thus to give

> them nothing. People who are creative are eager to strike out into new territory and to see, discover, and say what has not been seen, discovered, or said before. The writers and artists and editors of *The New Yorker* simply go where their own talent, imagination, energy, curiosity, and conscience take them.

Bill believed, and said, that the magazine reflected what he called "the light of principle," and it enabled its creators "to do their work against a stable background, in relative peace, and with absolute independence."

How he found the energy, the time, and the all-out devotion to do it all is inexplicable. But he did it. He continued doing it without giving up anything—or asking me to give up anything—in our full life together. There are scores of writers and artists and editors, including some still at *The New Yorker,* whose exceptional work can say what Bill Shawn gave them.

One of the most unusual writers Bill decided to corral was the late Hannah Arendt. Bill had a certain taste for her ideas. He read her books, all of which were beyond my field of interest. He told me about her penchant for having cozy evenings at her Riverside Drive apartment, with Susan Sontag, Mary McCarthy, and Jonathan Schell literally sitting at her feet, rapt, adoring, listening to her talk about political philosophy. Hannah Arendt pretending to be *Plato*? It all smacked to me of sanctimonious, narcissistic intellectualism. But I attributed my prejudices to my habitual suspicion of intellectuals in general, and I didn't say anything to Bill about them.

One day in late 1962 Bill informed me that Hannah Arendt herself had telephoned him and suggested to him that *The New Yorker* assign her to cover the trial of Adolf Eichmann, due to start soon in Israel. Eichmann was the Nazi war criminal who had been the principal mastermind of Hitler's program to exterminate the Jews. Bill told me shyly that he had decided to give Hannah Arendt the assignment. It sounded like a great idea, I said. Even if I had thought it was a bad idea, I would not have said so, because I never interfered with Bill in his job. I merely expressed my enjoyment on reading this or that in the magazine. It was a point of pride and honor to me to keep my place as a staff writer and not to overstep the line between writer and editorial authority.

So Hannah Arendt covered the trial and wrote a five-part piece about it, which became the book *Eichmann in Jerusalem.* The first part was published in the issue of February 16, 1963. Bill took on the job of editing it himself, no small job. The editing, he told me, would be unusually difficult, because it would be necessary to convert her often-cumbersome Germanic sentences into understandable prose. The piece, in which the writer coined the famous phrase "the banality of evil," caused a good deal of controversy, clamor, and protest. Among other things, Hannah Arendt was accused of having said that Jews themselves were culpable because they didn't resist the Nazis' efficient methods of using Jews as a way of organizing the extermination.

Bill didn't feel he should put Hannah Arendt to the inconvenience of coming to the office for the editing work, as all other writers did. Because of his respect for and awe of her, he insisted on going to her apartment, carrying, in addition to his customary briefcase and umbrella, fifty pounds or so of manuscript and proofs involved in the editing process. "It will make things easier for her," he said. The work, as all of us who have enjoyed the benefits of *The New Yorker*'s traditional editing procedures know, is tedious and challenging, and it requires enormous concentration, patience, and devotion to detail. It makes every writer sound better, much better. I happen to admire and enjoy it. It is so satisfying: clarity, logic, consistency, grammar, syntax, word repeats, devotion to the beauty of the English language—Bill and most of us who wrote for the magazine cared about all this. Every day, over a period of a few weeks, I would drop him off in a taxi—where we held hands, as we did automatically whenever we sat side by side—at Hannah Arendt's apartment on Riverside Drive. Hours later, I would come in a taxi to pick him up. He would be exhausted. Working with her was difficult, he told me, because of her difficulties with the English language. But she started out cooperatively. And he liked seeing her, although he found the apartment she shared with her husband—who taught political science, as she did, at nearby Columbia University—very dark, dismal, uncomfortable, and reeking of Mitteleuropean angst in decor and spirit. One day, shortly after starting to work with her, Bill emerged from the apartment, his face ashen. He was trembling. I took his hand. It was icy.

"As soon as she met me, she started on a strange rampage of anger and assault," he told me. "Nobody has ever talked to me like that. I don't understand it. She said our editing methods were a disgrace. She said they were 'stupid.' She demanded to know why she should be subjected to questioning. She didn't want to answer any more questions. She didn't want anything in her piece changed. She called me names, horrible names. I don't know what to do." He was shaking.

"Is she demented?" I asked. "Maybe something pushed her over the edge. Call Susan Sontag." I didn't know Susan Sontag, but I figured there might be something mysterious that only another high-powered intellectual could account for.

Bill shook his head miserably, in the negative. "She was so emotionally *violent,*" he said.

The next day I accompanied him as usual on the ride to Riverside Drive. His hand in mine felt clammy. He was pale and extremely nervous. "I don't know what to expect," he said, as he got out of the taxi. I helped carry the pounds of proofs and manuscripts to Hannah Arendt's lobby and left him at the elevator.

Three hours later I picked him up. He looked spacey. "She was O.K. Distant and cool, but O.K.," he said. "She answered all my questions. She acted as though nothing had happened. I don't understand it." He had a distant look, one that I had seen in him in previous retreats from violence and terror. I took his hand; again it was icy. "Until I can understand something with the rational side of my mind, I am tormented," he said, apologetically.

Almost every week Bill would tell me about some "amazing" talent he had just noticed or had just hired or with whom he had just planned some new piece of writing or art. Every time he rejoiced over a writer, an artist, or some element he was thrilled to publish in the magazine, he seemed to feel that the whole world would rejoice and be thrilled with him. That's the way he was. I noticed it soon after I joined the staff. The issue of August 31, 1946, for example—a date that happened to be his thirty-ninth birthday—was devoted to John Hersey's "Hiroshima," about the tragic effects on individuals in the city of the first atomic bombing in history. Bill had asked Hersey to do the reporting, and he worked with Hersey as he wrote the piece. It was Bill's idea to run it alone in the issue, without other editorial matter or cartoons; only the advertisements and the "Goings On" listings (*The Big Sleep, Brief Encounter,* and *Show Boat,* among others) were included. When the issue came out, Bill, looking bashful and tense, asked me to go to newsstands at Grand Central to see whether people were lining up to buy the magazine. I hurried over there and found no line, no crowd, only an atmosphere of business as usual. I returned to Bill and hesitantly gave him my report. He looked dismayed. "I thought that the entire town would be in an uproar," he said. "I thought they would be paying attention." By the next day, everybody indeed seemed to be paying attention to the horrifying story. It, too, became a book and a big seller.

Bill's interests were eclectic, and once he focused on a writer, an artist, an idea, or a plan, he went all out, giving everything that was in him to further the creation of that piece of writing, of that piece of art. He would stay the course with everybody, for all the weeks or months or years it took to come up with what he wanted to publish. And everybody who had that experience with him would feel the exhilaration of seeming to be the single object of his love, without the complication of being expected to give anything in return except their creation. And they were made to feel that they had wrought the marvels—short or long—all by themselves.

That is how it was, for example, with John Updike, who started as a "Talk of the Town" reporter, and wrote "Rockefeller Center Ho!" (2/11/56) before moving to New England to concentrate not only on his fiction but on a prodigious outpouring of other work. Or Roger Angell—the incomparable writer about baseball and an incomparable fiction editor, continuing the tradition of the dedicated Katharine S. White, who happened to be his mother—who succeeded Frank Sullivan as the author of the annual Christmas poem and wrote his first one, "Greetings, Friends!," for the 12/27/76 issue. Or Ian Frazier, a very young writer whose exceptional quality Bill recognized immediately, with Frazier's first offering, a Talk story, "Decorative Value" (4/15/74). Mark Singer was another writer, like Frazier, of the younger generation, which Bill considered so important for the future of the magazine.

Bill was enthusiastic about every new writer, but particularly so about the young ones. One evening in the mid 1960s, while watching PBS's Channel 13, we spotted Hendrik Hertzberg, then a recent college graduate, in a group discussion about "commitment." Bill immediately got in touch with him and hired him as a staff reporter. Hertzberg has been "committed"—to clear thinking and original writing—ever since. When a young John McPhee came to Bill and said he wanted to know more about *The New Yorker*'s reporting, Bill let him sit hour after hour in his office, asking questions and making meticulous notes; he returned again and again for more, and then came up with reporting that has been astonishing readers for over thirty years—for example, "The Headmaster" (3/19/66) and "Levels of the Game" (6/7/69 and 6/14/69).

Then there was W. H. Auden. Bill would take him to lunch, listen to him talk about his life in New York, his loves, his hopes, his pain, and then come back to the office, drop in on me, and try to compose himself before returning to his own desk. Auden contributed thirty poems, as well as dozens of Books pieces, including his last one, about *The Letters of Anton Chekhov* (9/3/73). Mollie Panter-Downs, a quiet, down-to-earth, poetic writer, steadily sent in her "Letter from London" throughout World War II, and wrote various pieces for the magazine until 1984. There was V. S. Pritchett, whom Bill considered the finest of the literary critics. When Bill received a piece from him, he would telephone thanks to Pritchett, and follow that up with a letter of appreciation. Berton Roueché worked at first for Bill as an editor and then turned his exceptional gifts to his own prose, writing the first of what would be fifty-eight "Annals of Medicine" pieces, "The Case of the Eleven Blue Men" (6/5/48). The artist Saul Steinberg was, in Bill's opinion, the greatest living artist next to Picasso. Sixty-eight of his covers appeared on *The New Yorker* between 1945 and 1986, including the famous one depicting the United States as New York City, with all the rest of the country foreshortened to a slivered West Coast. And there was the brilliantly encyclocinematic Pauline Kael, whose passionate criticisms and crusades kept Bill, for the most part, enthralled.

I used to read college newspapers for Bill to see what the young journalists were up to, and in the *The Harvard Crimson* one day I spotted some reports by its editor, Bill McKibben, and told Bill Shawn about him. Bill telephoned him, by chance on April Fool's Day; McKibben thought it was a joke and didn't return the call. Bill was hurt and thought that McKibben wasn't *interested* in the magazine. I couldn't believe that. With some prodding from me, Bill called again and this time reached McKibben, who came to see Bill and soon was writing funny stories for "The Talk of the Town"—for instance, "Bojangles'" (10/4/82). Again, Bill thought he had a candidate to train as a successor. But this young man also seemed to have too much talent as a writer to give it up in the service of other writers.

There was Thomas Whiteside, who wrote many solid reporting pieces, including a warning about Agent Orange, a defoliant used in the Vietnam War. There was Philip Hamburger, who for decades provided consistently original Profiles—among others, one of Mayor William O'Dwyer, "That Great Big New York Up There" (9/28/57). Bill was enchanted by brilliant, beautiful, eager young women, such as Renata Adler, who came to him in 1962 and offered, he told me, "to wash the floors or do anything" at *The New Yorker.* He wanted her to write—with her distinctive, extraordinary prose—some literary criticism, but she wanted to turn to reporting and went to Selma, Alabama, to cover the famous civil rights march ("Letter from Selma," 4/10/65). Maeve Brennan had come to the United States at the age of seventeen with her father, Ireland's envoy to Washington. Bill hired her to write about fashion, and then discovered that she could write true, funny, sad, and moving short stories about Dublin life, like "The Clever One" (5/30/53). Bill was enchanted by her and her Dublin accent, called her "a fairy princess," and continually found excuses to drop in at her office. She wrote many poignant, funny pieces, published in "The Talk of the Town" as "Communications from a Long-Winded Lady" (1954–1981). And he was also spellbound by brilliant, beautiful Jane Kramer, who wrote wonderful Talk stories and then took over the late Janet Flanner's position in Paris, sending in a frequent "Letter from Europe." And he would be charmed by Jamaica Kincaid, when she wrote a superb piece, during Christmas week, about her father, a carpenter (Comment, 1/3/83).

His deep feeling wasn't confined to women. It extended to many men, such as Calvin Trillin, in my opinion one of the best reporters of our time, who wrote one of the best reporting pieces of our time, about a young American student who contracted a disease in China and died there ("Zei-Da-Man," 10/7/85). Bill would feel triumphant every time he was able to wrest Bruce McCall away from doing advertisements for Mercedes to writing humor pieces for *The New Yorker.* He would feel doubly triumphant and joyous every time he received an offering from that very original, very funny artist Roz Chast. Every now and then, he would feel that a genius had entered his domain, and he would be awed by that. For instance, George W. S. Trow, a highly temperamental young man, seemed to have difficulty in communicating with most people, but not with Bill, who was able to shift gears and adjust to anyone else's mind. Bill was very excited by Trow's ideas about what was transpiring in our culture, and the two of them closeted themselves for days, talking about the essay Trow was writing on the subject. When it was published, Bill was as proud of Trow's essay, "Within the Context of No Context" (11/17/80), as he had been of anything since "Hiroshima."

It was with Jonathan Schell that Bill collaborated over a period of about twenty years in writing, week after week, about important political matters of the time—the Vietnam War, the Nixon years and Watergate, and the menace—the imminent menace, they felt—of nuclear war. They would do considerable talking about the content, then Schell would write a draft, and together they would revise and finish it. They took the work with the utmost seriousness. One week, in the spring of 1973, Bill sent Schell to Washington. Upon returning, Schell wrote a Comment quoting one politician as saying, "Today the whole Constitution is up for grabs" (4/28/1973). In 1982, their collaboration reached a kind of crescendo, as Schell worked on what became the book *The Fate of the Earth.* When Part I of the three-part piece was about to appear ("A Republic of Insects and Grass," 2/1/82), Bill came into my office looking distraught. "When the magazine comes out, I fear that people are going to be running hysterically through the streets," he said. The effect wasn't quite that dramatic, but Schell's book, which became a best-seller, did make a terrific impact on people's awareness of what would happen in the event of nuclear war.

The aforementioned contributors are only a small sampling of the scores of people whose lives were intertwined with the life of Bill Shawn in their work.

When Bill and I sat together in his office to go over the editing of my stories, we worked seriously and professionally, but the atmosphere of love was not suspended; it enhanced the pleasure that we shared in our work.

Over the fifty-odd years that Bill Shawn worked with scores and scores of talented people of one sort or another, he accommodated himself, as I have said, to their vocabularies, to their rhythms, and to their endless needs. "Nobody else can do what you can do," he would repeatedly tell his writers. He went about his work with speed, courtesy, and concentration. His feelings for his writers and artists were revealed, among other things, in the way he worked on the proofs of their writing, as he prepared it for publication. A proof, bearing the perfect symmetry of his small handwriting, along with the traditional proofreading marks, became a thing of visual beauty. He cared about the way his commas looked. He never lost this special touch. In his eighties, he still preferred to work on unlined white sheets of eight-by-ten-inch paper, using a blue ballpoint pen. His handwriting was impeccably even, all the way down the page. It never changed.

As editors, Ross and Shawn were alike in many surprising ways. They shared a belief in the importance of shielding writers from disturbances. It was assumed that the editors would bear something akin to a parental role in their dealings with the staff. As soon as Ross had Shawn to depend on, Ross could escape the brunt of such a role and most of the abuse that went with it. He responded to trouble with a certain amount of waving of his arms, even at those icons Thurber, White, et al. But Shawn sat and took the batterings. He did not know how to duck. Harold Ross may have had some cranky, politically conservative inclinations, but he was enormously respectful of his managing editor. And Bill Shawn understood and appreciated not only the genius of Harold Ross but the inner nature of Harold Ross.

When the writer Brendan Gill was completing his book *Here at The New Yorker* in 1975, Bill Shawn worried that Gill would not be able to give a true picture of Ross, so he offered to write what turned out to be an almost four-thousand-word essay about the founding editor for inclusion in the book. Gill included it as written. This is how Shawn began the essay:

> Harold Ross presented himself to the world as a raucous, clumsy, primitive, somewhat comic figure. He said extremely funny things spontaneously and intentionally, and in his conversation and in his physical bearing he was funny unintentionally, or almost unintentionally, as well. He lent himself to anecdote. Because of this, and because his personal qualities were large in scale and included a formidable charm and magnetism, the serious and inspired work that he did as an editor tended at times to be lost sight of. Occasionally, when contemporaries of Ross talked about the old days on *The New Yorker,* one got the impression that he did very little to create it or run it—that in spite of his inadequacies, and somehow over his protest, a number of other people did what was nec-

essary to put out the magazine each week. The implication was that Ross spent much of his time getting in the way of the talented people who worked for him. None of this, of course, is true.

Bill Shawn went on to describe many aspects of Ross. "Ross was an enormously intelligent man who worked almost entirely by instinct and intuition," he wrote, and "Of Ross's own qualities, perhaps the most important was his honesty. The idea of distorting information, of tampering with facts, of saying something that you knew was incorrect or that you didn't mean, repelled him." Gill used the essay as the ending to his book, with an additional note saying "Shawn on Ross—yes, but one perceives that it is Shawn on Shawn as well."

Bill had the ability to draw an uncrossable line between his secret self and most other people while simultaneously responding to people in a close, mindful, and sympathetic way. To my knowledge, he never let anybody down, no matter what the problem—illness, death, divorce, difficulties with children, difficulties with parents, difficulties with wives or husbands, finances, alcoholism, loneliness, nervous breakdowns, jealousies of other writers or artists, writer's block. Without complaint, he would salvage a story here and a story there, and always, thinking about the life of the writer or artist, he would try to salvage his self-respect. Bill would howl in frustration, however, when a mediocre writer, believing in his own "greatness," would become, over the years, more and more mediocre—and somehow, more and more troublesome. It would be the mediocre writer who fancied himself "great," Bill would point out to me, who would feel free to complain publicly about the magazine—knowing full well that Bill never acted vengefully toward anybody. The great writers, not feeling the need to announce their own greatness, remained quietly at work. Occasionally, some writers might try to interfere with Bill's judgment about the work of other writers. They might threaten to resign, or might make public statements about how unhappy Harold Ross would be if he were still alive. Such attempts to take possession of the previous editor were dismaying to Bill. He often explained to me that he sometimes felt he *had* to publish this or that for his own good reasons, but he never changed his judgment because of pressure from a jealous or bitter writer.

Bill stubbornly went to bat for a writer he believed in, even when Harold Ross or, in later years, others, did not see what Bill understood about a writer. When he was managing editor, he told me, years before I came to the magazine, Harold Ross had wanted to fire A. J. Liebling, claiming, "He can't write anything." Bill laughed as he told me that. He knew that Liebling had the potential to become a marvelous writer, so he worked with him and worked with him, and A. J. Liebling did indeed become a marvelous writer.

In 1961, J. D. Salinger sent Bill his story "Zooey." Bill was excited by its originality and power. To his dismay, however, the editors in the fiction department did not like it and wanted to reject it. Bill showed me their written opinions and told me he was going to ignore them and publish the story, which went on to become a classic. (Written opinions of fiction were supposed to be kept on file in the office; by mistake, the "Zooey" opinions were sent to Salinger, he told me, when his manuscript was returned to him after the story was published!)

After World War II, in 1947, *The New Yorker Book of War Pieces* was published, quietly, without fanfare. Bill told me he had assigned every one of the pieces in the book, had edited every one for the magazine, and then had compiled the book without putting his own name on it. The dedication reads:

TO THE MEMORY OF

DAVID LARDNER

KILLED AT AACHEN, OCTOBER 18, 1944

The jacket copy he wrote reads: "*The New Yorker* Book of War Pieces—from London, September 2, 1939, to Hiroshima, August 6, 1945. Selected and Arranged with the Assistance of the Editors of *The New Yorker*." Every piece in the book was a model of reporting—fresh, original, exciting, moving, journalistically instructive. Colonel Joseph J. Green of the *Infantry Journal* was quoted on the back of the book jacket: "One magazine of general circulation stands high above all others in accuracy of what it printed about the war—*The New Yorker*. Its score isn't perfect, but week after week, it printed articles and stories dealing with many different sides of the Armed Services, which showed the most careful editorial supervision to see that nothing remotely approaching the phony was included. The stuff not only stacked up high in literary merit; it also showed American readers what the Army, the Navy, the Marines, are actually like, whether in battle action or barracks service. There was not one line of gee-whiz."

The New Yorker would not keep quiet about Vietnam, no matter how many people, including advertisers, complained. Bill's fearfulness, expressed in his phobias, did not extend to the principles he followed in setting policies for the magazine. *The New Yorker* would not be quiet about the years with Richard Nixon in this country. Once, and only once, the publisher, Peter Fleischmann, came up from the business floor (editorial and business activities were conducted on different floors, and starting with Harold Ross, business people were told firmly not to appear on the editorial floor) and came to Bill's office. To Bill's astonishment and anger, Mr. Fleischmann asked him not to publish something. It was 1970. The "something" was the artist James Stevenson's satirical spread on Spiro Agnew and the Nixon administration. Bill told Mr. Fleischmann that he was going to go ahead and publish the spread. A few days later, the two men met for lunch outside the office. Mr. Fleischmann told Bill he thought the magazine was becoming too much of a "political journal," and he asked

Bill if he, the owner and publisher, was being told to "stay out" of editorial affairs. Yes, Bill said very gently, that is exactly what he was being told. Thereafter, Peter Fleischmann never again came up to the editorial floor. The two men remained friends, and Bill admired and respected Peter Fleischmann for having the strength of character to back off. And also, Bill told me, Peter Fleischmann supported the magazine in what Bill called "the strong, dangerous stand we were taking editorially on Vietnam and the Nixon administration, long before Agnew's resignation and long before Watergate."

One year, in the early 1960s, I wrote a series of twenty-one short Profiles of actors in an effort to get at some of the intriguing secrets of what makes an actor. Bill and I shared an enthusiasm for actors and acting. Working on the Profiles was a happy experience for us. After the pieces were published in *The New Yorker,* I enlisted the help of my sister, Helen, who felt as we did about actors, in doing additional Profiles. Together, Bill said, the pieces made "a profile of an art." The pieces then appeared as a book, which we called *The Player,* subtitled "A Profile of an Art," and to our satisfaction, it was widely read by actors. To this day, I'm told, actors seek it out in bookshops. Each Profile began with a quote from the actor; the theme of the book was stated by Kim Stanley, who said: "Unlike other artists, the actor has only his own body and his own self to work with. To exhibit oneself on the stage is quite a brave and wonderful thing to do." What she had to say, along with what we were told by Paul Scofield, Jane Fonda, Henry Fonda, Anthony Quinn, Paul Newman, John Gielgud, Walter Matthau, Angela Lansbury, Warren Beatty, Katharine Cornell, Sidney Poitier, Sophia Loren, and forty-three others, made Helen, Bill, and me love and admire actors more than ever. I took most of the photographs for the book and heard no complaints. When I ran into Angela Lansbury, a good thirty-five years after the book was published, she reminded me that her lead-off quote was "When I'm onstage, I often think, What the hell am I doing here? I realize that I want to go home." She added, with a laugh, "I still feel that way."

A couple of television producers were eager to put *The Player* on television. Helen and I responded enthusiastically to the idea. Our way of doing it, we said, would be to use the same format as the book's: present each actor in close-up talking about his art. Just that. The television producers said that a television audience would not be satisfied with just that. Other visuals would have to be included—film or video clips from their plays or movies, childhood photographs, music, critical commentaries, and so forth. We said no. Our foray into television was aborted.

Most of the writers and artists on the *New Yorker* staff, a diverse, opinionated, volatile, and egotistical group, were at one with one another only in their view of Bill Shawn. He understood them; he appreciated them; he alone knew what special marvels they were. He wanted to give *them* what *they* wanted. His saying "Nobody else can do what *you* can do," no matter how often it was repeated, was always welcome. There were many elements, I believe, that went into the use of the word "legendary" about Bill Shawn. For one thing, he was genuinely democratic. In the restaurants he frequented, he always shook hands with all the (usually "invisible") busboys, as well as with the maître d's. He would see anybody, anybody at all, who wrote to him as the editor-in-chief, and asked to be seen. Nevertheless, to the outside world, and to most in the literary and publishing world, he was "Mr. Shawn." His name was spoken with the utmost respect and even awe. One day in 1988, about a year after Bill left *The New Yorker*, we were strolling along Fifty-seventh Street near the Russian Tea Room when we ran into the agent Sam Cohn, who was "legendary" in his own right. Mr. Cohn, only a couple of decades younger than Bill Shawn, bowed as the two men shook hands, and Mr. Cohn said, in a heartfelt way, "How are you, sir?" The "sir" made Bill Shawn blush.

Bill Shawn was criticized mostly, it seemed, for being too indulgent with his writers. Some critics berated him for discouraging writers from using obscene words. In private, he was very earthy, and he used his share of obscenities. But he felt a kind of compulsive, gentlemanly protectiveness toward his readers. What concerned him was the bigger issue of unnecessary cruelty and destructiveness. Also, in his literary judgment, jarring, shortcut words fell short of perfection in writing, and he was always striving for "perfection." "I will go to a concert given by the Italian Quartet in order to remind myself how far short of perfection the magazine still is," he once said to me. He recognized the validity of the obscenities in the writing of James Joyce, but he did not consider most of the fiction writers he published in his magazine to be in a class with Joyce. Beyond all that, he regretted ugliness in all forms, and in his view obscenities were ugly. Some writers, during literary disagreements, would angrily accuse Bill of being "squeamish" or "old-fashioned." His feelings might be hurt by their criticism, but he never attempted to defend himself. I accompanied him to some pornographic movies, and his only objection to them was their inept direction, acting, and cinematography. He was never patronizing or condescending with a writer or an artist. Once I told him about an interview during which I was asked to name the books that had most influenced me. *The Bobbsey Twins* and *The Five Little Peppers,* I said, thus shocking and apparently disappointing the interviewer. Bill laughed appreciatively and said that *The Five Little Peppers* had also been one of his favorites.

Pundits have spoken over the ages about the egomaniacal writer-artist, so I am saying very little when I say that writers are not necessarily far removed from their childish natures. In observing writers over the past fifty years—at *The New Yorker* and nearby—I have noticed that their frustration or disappointment in themselves is often revealed in the way they strike out at the very individuals or institutions who have been the most helpful to them. Children, of course, do that all the time with their parents. It seems at times that writers who are in trouble with themselves and with their writing go on the attack against people who have the misfortune of occupying a parental role. Jealousy and rage then replace creative energy in the writer. If a writer is busily engaging his energies in his own work, Bill Shawn used to tell me, that writer is not looking for anyone to blame for his miseries; there is nobody and nothing to be jealous of. If one were to make a list of the writers and artists who have been giving their time and attention in the past few years to attacks on other writers or artists, one might well find a list of writers and artists who are in deep trouble with themselves.

One writer for whom I have the deepest respect and admiration is J. D. Salinger. He has never been publicly hostile to other writers or joined in any of the self-serving publicity and game-playing politics that seem to be rather generic in the literary world. For some reason, it takes almost superhuman strength of character and purpose these days to do what Salinger seems to do: he stays put and writes. Instead of eliciting praise for his lonely and courageous course, he has been put down, sniped at, attacked by some other writers, and resented for not joining in the fray. He has also been resented for passing up what is "everything" to some writers—all the way from the obligatory appearances on television talk shows to the zillion-dollar sale of a book to Hollywood. Some writers may yearn for these perks, and I can understand that. I, too, like the perks. There are practical rationalizations for all of them. What I don't understand is why some writers will not accept the fact that J. D. Salinger may not *want* what *they* want. He is such a unique and powerful and funny writer. Like

Marlon Brando, he is also a rare figure among all artists. On the human side, Salinger has, among other things, managed to do what so many (apparently necessarily) self-centered others have failed to do—that is, to be a solid and responsible parent to his children.

In the 1950s, Bill introduced me to Salinger, and the three of us would have dinner together when he came down from his home in New Hampshire. He was always charming, funny, open, direct, and seemingly simple. Of all the scores of writers Bill dealt with over the years, including some who were old friends, only Salinger would go out of his way to be helpful to Bill without asking for anything in return. When it comes to writing, along with what Bill taught me, I've learned the most from Salinger. He's one of the best we've ever had.

When Salinger's book *Franny and Zooey,* which had appeared first as two long stories in *The New Yorker,* was published, Bill was surprised and moved to find it was dedicated to him: "As nearly as possible in the spirit of Matthew Salinger, age one, urging a luncheon companion to accept a cool lima bean, I urge my editor, mentor, and (heaven help him) closest friend, William Shawn, *genius domus* of *The New Yorker,* lover of the long shot, protector of the unprolific, defender of the hopelessly flamboyant, most unreasonably modest of born great artist editors, to accept this pretty skimpy-looking book."

Bill has had some public recognition—in a quiet way—for having been on what would today be called "the cutting edge." Often mentioned is his publishing John Hersey's "Hiroshima" alone in the magazine, without any cartoons, in order to focus attention on the dangers of nuclear warfare. But his innovations were steady throughout his editorship. Bill startled the magazine's advertising people and the advertising world in general by making it a magazine policy to refuse to run advertising for cigarettes. In 1962, *The New Yorker* and Bill were attacked by many other publications, including *Time* magazine, for publishing Rachel Carson's "Silent Spring," the first major warning about the poisoning of our lands. *Time* magazine called "Silent Spring" "unfair, one-sided, and hysterically over-emphatic," and accused Carson of frightening the public with "emotion-fanning words." Later published as a book, it went on to become a best-seller all over the world, and was followed by other Rachel Carson writings about the many dangers to our environment. Bill was eagerly on the lookout for the new and always open to it. When Ingmar Bergman's agent sent me a copy of the Swedish moviemaker's screenplay *Cries and Whispers,* I gave it to Bill, who decided at once that it had extraordinary literary merit, and he published it. There is a long list on Bill Shawn's record of literary and journalistic firsts, including James Baldwin's famous and explosive "The Fire Next Time." Bill published it as a "Letter from a Region in My Mind" in the issue of November 17, 1962, a time when the expression of such passionate moral outrage over racism was unprecedented.

In 1993, when I returned to *The New Yorker* to write for Tina Brown, people both inside and outside the magazine asked me how I "felt" about her. I found the questions superfluous. By coming to work for her, wasn't I making it clear how I felt? It was what I wanted to do. To me, as I have said, the magazine has always been an expression of the person who creates it by knowing how to find and use talented artists and writers. Tina Brown, like Bill Shawn, was doing just that. She knew how to "connect" with talent. The uniqueness of Bill Shawn's soul and spirit may never be duplicated. But I found Tina Brown, in her own way, interesting and impressive, especially given her youth. Moreover, I found that she possessed—under the usual disguises—her own share of Bill's kind of naivety, insight, and sensitivity, and, what's more, her own hunger for wit and humor. She, too, "got it." It's too bad that Bill didn't have a chance to work with her. Si

Newhouse gave her the job on August 31, 1992, Bill's eighty-fifth birthday. Her first issue came out on the following October 6.

I think it's impossible to keep a magazine, especially a weekly magazine, consistent in quality. I was often bored by, or impatient with, or disapproving of, pieces, fiction and nonfiction, in Bill Shawn's *New Yorker.* And Bill Shawn felt the same lack of pleasure in some of what he was responsible for publishing. But I invariably found at least one or two elements in each issue of his magazine that were intriguing or admirable or thrilling. The same is true of Tina Brown's *New Yorker.* Tina Brown's editorial ideas were challenging to me as a writer. As a small example, she wanted "Talk of the Town" stories to be half the length they were twenty or thirty years earlier. To me that was a difficult and welcome challenge. And again, for me, it was fun.

My colleagues on the staff today continue to interest and inspire me, as they did fifty years ago. The staff still includes writers who worked with Bill Shawn—irreplaceable writers such as Susan Sheehan, Mark Singer, Calvin Tomkins, John Updike, Nancy Franklin, William Finnegan, John McPhee, Philip Hamburger, Roger Angell, Arlene Croce, Janet Malcolm, Lawrence Weschler, Calvin Trillin, Jane Kramer, Alec Wilkinson, Whitney Balliett, and Hendrik Hertzberg. Some of them are better than ever. Among the new crop—the heirs to Joe Mitchell and Joe Liebling—are David Remnick, Philip Gourevitch, John Lahr, Henry Louis Gates, Jr., Peter Boyer, Hilton Als, Ken Auletta, Alison Rose, John Seabrook, Jeffrey Toobin, Susan Orlean, Malcolm Gladwell, Jane Mayer, and the amazing young (early thirties) Anthony Lane, who is, I think as thrilling and instructive to read as Wolcott Gibbs was in my early years at the magazine. It's also fun for me to read the work of, say, John Seabrook, another thirty-something, and to see *him,* with each new piece, raise his writing to a higher level. Some talented women in quiet roles during Bill

Shawn's time have blossomed noticeably with Tina Brown at the helm—for example, the poet and editor Deborah Garrison, and those two exceptional and exceptionally funny writers, Nancy Franklin and Alison Rose. *The New Yorker*'s tradition of finding and nurturing talent clearly continues. Part of my enjoyment, of course, comes from identifying in today's reporting and writing in *The New Yorker* echoes of literary legacies established over the years by writers whose names so many of us from the magazine will never forget—Wolcott Gibbs, James Thurber, E. B. White, S. J. Perelman, John McCarten, Mark Murphy, John Lardner, Susan Lardner, Daniel Lang, Brendan Gill, Maeve Brennan, Geoffrey Hellman, Richard Rovere, Janet Flanner, Mollie Panter-Downs, Edmund Wilson, Pauline Kael, Harold Rosenberg, Berton Roueché, John Hersey, Janet Malcolm, Joseph Mitchell, A. J. Liebling, Jonathan Schell, Jane Kramer, Roger Angell, Andy Logan, John McPhee, Tony Hiss, Mark Singer, and fiction writers J. D. Salinger, John Cheever, and Donald Barthelme, among others. The staff writers who originally influenced and inspired me were A. J. Liebling and Joseph Mitchell.

All writers, of course, have needed the one called the "editor," who singularly, almost mystically, embodies the many-faceted, unique life force infusing the entire enchilada. And surprising as it may seem on the surface, William Shawn and Tina Brown, the current editor, are indeed similar. Bill Shawn often talked to me about how much he wanted to have exquisite photography in the magazine, but his then art editor, James Geraghty, was opposed to it, so Bill sadly gave up. He longed to use true colors in the pages, but he was persuaded to retreat from this idea, too. Tina Brown wanted the photography of Richard Avedon and others, and she wanted color, and she put what she wanted in the magazine. She, too, in many ways, has been giving *The New Yorker* "several new dimensions" and has been "broadening its journalistic scope." Bill Shawn's one-of-a-kind artists Robert Mankoff, Warren

Miller, Robert Weber, Frank Modell, Arnie Levin, George Booth, Jack Ziegler, Ed Koren, Roz Chast, and Saul Steinberg are now joined in *The New Yorker* by Tina Brown's crew, and I happen to find it delightful to see the work of the genius William Steig (age ninety) in the pages of the magazine along with the work of the genius Art Spiegelman (half that). For me, it's all adrenaline.

For Bill, I wrote what I wanted to write. I discovered, early on, that I usually did not want to write about anyone I did not like. I also began to develop the belief that I would get a sense of the person I was going to write about in the first few minutes of our meeting, and it would invariably be that sense of the person that would guide me in what I wrote. Then I found—and I set down some of these ideas in an introduction I wrote to a new edition of *Reporting,* a collection of my reporting pieces that included "Portrait of Hemingway"—that one's obligation to the people one wrote about did not end once the writing was published. I still firmly believe, as I said there, that anyone who trusts you enough to talk about himself to you is giving you a form of friendship, and if you spend weeks or months with someone, not only taking his time and energy but entering into his life, you naturally become his friend. A friend is not to be used or abandoned; the friendship established in writing about someone usually continues to grow after what has been written is published.

I discovered that my friendships with people I'd written about were two-sided. Even a few of the Indiana Bean Blossom High School students I'd written about in 1960 in "The Yellow Bus" have continued to keep me posted on their lives. In that story, for example, I quoted, among the mainly unresponsive-to-and-suspicious-of-New York students, a "Becky Kiser" ("Becky Kiser, with an expression of terrible guilt on her attractive, wide-mouthed face, said, 'I bet you'd never get bored here in New York. Back home, it's the same thing all the time. You go to the skating rink. You go to the Big Boy. In the winter, there's basketball. And that's all.' ") Recently—thirty-seven years later—Becky Kiser came to New York and left a message for me saying she'd like to get together and bring me up to date on the Bean Blossomers. Unfortunately, by the time I received the message, she had checked out of her hotel.

My friendship with John Huston and his family continued for years after I had initially written about him in *Picture.* He and his late wife, Ricki, became close friends of mine. In 1987, a few days before he died, he left a telephone message for me and my son, Erik, on our answering machine: "Don't worry about me, darlings," he said, in his strong, mellifluous voice. "I'm just *fine.*" When his daughter Anjelica started directing her first movie in 1995, it gave me considerable pleasure to visit her on location and write about her. ("I didn't want to do more *Prizzi's Honor. Prizzi's Honor* belongs to Dad. I want to do something of my own.")

William Faulkner, whom I had met in Hollywood, while he was working unhappily on screenplay writing, used to drop in on me in my office in New York and sit around, chatting about his problems with alcohol. With considerable humor, he described a New York Center where he went for treatment for his alcoholism. He gave me some short stories about alcoholism, and I sent them along to the fiction department, whose editors decided against publishing them. This kind of exposure to the lives of the famous showed me over and over again that I wanted, for myself, a quieter more modest life.

When I wrote a Talk story about Robin Williams (I went with him in 1984 to a New York comedy club and caught him in the process of inventing his "Dr. Rufe" routine), he and his wife-to-be, Marsha Garces, began a friendship with me. I shared all of these friendships and many more with Bill, who looked forward eagerly to the distraction of lighthearted dinners with them and always took these "stars" on their own terms. In 1993, writing for Tina Brown, I did a Profile of the Williamses, describing the making of the movie *Mrs. Doubtfire,* with Marsha as the overall producer. The role of observer is my natural role and I have never fully retreated from it, but I think that as an observer I have the same capacity for loyalty, joy, and love as any engaged participant.

Writing for *The New Yorker* was a full and satisfying and constantly joyous way of life. I had loved journalism; now I adored it. I was thrilled and inspired by the journalism of my colleagues, and I reveled in their generosity of spirit when they complimented me. I find myself going through exactly the same experience now. Reading the work of the uniquely talented people—powerhouse writers, so many of them, and half my age—inspires me to intensify the quality of my own offerings. Some of my recent Talk stories—"The Shit-Kickers of Madison Avenue" (about fifteen-year-old school-girls talking and smoking and eating French fries and planning a party), "The Golden Ladies of the Golden Door" (about forty ladies spending a week together at a famous California spa), "Looking Out for 'Number One' " (about Jackson Pollock's painting of that name put up for sale by Frank Stanton, who was William Paley's well-known Number Two), "Postpartum Dept." (about young mothers marking time with their babies but impatient to return to their jobs), and "The Sporting Scene" (about John McEnroe in his incarnation as a television sportscaster)—have been just as much fun for me to do as the old ones. I never wanted to write *War and Peace.* I never wanted to comment on the state of the universe. I never wanted to do what any other writer was doing. I wanted what I still want: to write my own little stories.

CHAPTER 9

ERIK

As my life with Bill went along, I never felt deprived of anything I wanted. However, by the 1960s (our tenth anniversary by our own way of counting) I realized that I was doing less and less of the reporting and the writing I loved. I had my fans and admirers, who would write to me and ask me why they hadn't found any writing by me in the magazine. When I emerged socially, people would ask me the same question. From time to time, I asked myself that question. I didn't seem to care as passionately, as wholeheartedly, as I once had cared about writing. Was I being deprived of it by anyone but myself? Bill kept urging me to get to work, to write the stories I had already reported but hadn't written. No one was stopping me. I simply didn't have the drive that had been with me all my life. I was surprising myself. Also, Bill had told me so much about his grieving and worrying and life-giving to a multitude of writers that I began to feel guilty. I questioned my own character. Was I just another greedy, selfish, self-serving writer? I would tell myself quickly that I was not. But I was questioning the big decision I had made about what I was doing with my life. I had loved being a reporter. I had lived for it. But something stronger in me was making me give it up. If a Talk assignment came my way, I would get up the enthusiasm to do it, but I was letting months go by without doing the long pieces that I should have been writing. By the late 1960s, my priorities had quietly shifted. Instead of thinking about my work, I was spending days and nights thinking about what women like to think about—a baby. I talked to Bill about it, and he was immediately sympathetic.

I had been fascinated with babies ever since I was a small child, perhaps because of Teddy. When Bill and I took walks together on the street, we would play a game in which we challenged each other to make eye contact with, and communicate with, any baby in a carriage approaching from half a block away. I always won. Once I scared Bill by writing a short story about a young woman in a supermarket, planning to kidnap the baby of a mean mother. I reassured Bill that it was only fiction. (The story was rejected.) Children in general were interesting to me. In the 1970s, I did a study, on a Guggenheim fellowship, about the meaning of children's play. One year, I wrote and directed a documentary movie, *Dancers in May,* about a teacher at a Lower East Side public school preparing fifth- and sixth-graders to participate in a dance festival in Central Park. Simultaneously, I wrote a piece about it, also called "Dancers in May," for *The New Yorker.* Bill gave both the story and the movie their title. The movie was shown on Channel 13. Before the showing, *The New York Times* asked me to do a piece about the writing of my story *cum* the making of the film. They gave me a lot of space. Among other things, I wrote: "In doing this story, I found, as I've found in some others I've written (including fiction), that at a certain point the characters took over and more or less arranged everything themselves, so that all I had to do was see it and hear it and write it down. Add 'and catch it on film,' and you have a description of how the story became a television movie."

Our movie reviews were good.

It was an interesting journalistic experiment, and I loved working with those kids. In taking leave of them, on impulse, I gave one of them my clarinet.

Bill and I considered having a biological child together, despite the ramifications, in the 1960s, of taking that step. Then fate intervened. I had been repeatedly delaying surgery to remove fibroid tumors in order to prepare for pregnancy, and having delayed too long, I was compelled to have a hysterectomy. I was amazed by my philosophical acceptance of this tragedy. Bill seemed to be more distraught about it than I was.

My next step was to find a baby to adopt. One day, Bill saw in a magazine a photograph of a baby in Burma. We started thinking about my going to Burma. Bill said perhaps we might start the search for a Burmese baby by advertising in a Burmese newspaper. I immediately placed such an ad. I got only one reply. "I am a man, sad and alone, thirty-eight years of age and wish you to adopt me," it began. We decided I should not go to Burma.

I searched around here and there in this country, finding obstacles of one kind or another. In 1965, a friend working in Norway happened to mention to me that an unmarried Norwegian woman he knew had recently had a child, and because of their socialized medical system, together with their relaxed attitude in the matter, at least in Oslo, everybody concerned was very happy about this addition to their country's population. Norway sounded good to me. *Commandos Strike at Dawn,* in which Paul Muni, playing a hero of the Norwegian underground, destroyed a power plant where the Germans were producing materials for an atomic bomb, had made me cry. I never forgot it. Paul Muni's girlfriend and his mother helped him fight the Nazis, and he was killed in the end. So I went to Norway. By now, I knew how to use the word "beautiful." The country was beautiful. Everybody walking on the streets in Oslo looked beautiful, too. The king was beautiful. It was a fairy-tale country, with a benevolent, affectionate king who democratically went cross-country skiing on the Oslo trails with his people. Along with satisfied, smiling parents of little boys and girls, I attended a ceremony at a fjord where the king gave out sailing awards to every child. I loved the way the king shook hands with the children and the way the children shook hands with him. When the king needed a cataract operation, he was offered priority on the list of people signed up for it, but he refused, saying he would wait his turn. My kind of king.

Everybody in the shops looked strong and healthy and purposeful and brave. Every baby in sight had plump, red cheeks and eyes like Teddy's and Bill's. Also, Norway up there at the top abuts Russia, where my roots are, and I liked the idea of roots. My cousin Henry Rosovsky, former longtime dean at Harvard and Geyser University Professor Emeritus at Harvard, tells me that the family name Rosovsky, which was mine, means "forest of trees," and that we are all inbred and have been marrying each other for generations. The inbreeding, he says, seems to have done things for our life span. His mother's great-grandmother, for instance, died at the age of one hundred and seven. I asked him, for a Talk story I wanted to write, if she had eaten yogurt. "No, she drank vodka," he said. All in all, I felt it was just as well for me to go the adoption route.

Everything moved magically (Bill's word) in my adoption of the baby. I talked to Agnes Haug, a judge in the Ministry of Justice with authority in adoptions. She told me that if I was able to locate a baby, she would see what she could do to help. My friend had a friend who knew about a baby due to be born in about five months, and I met the social worker in the case. She looked like a young Greta Garbo, but warmer, more sympathetic. She said she would see what she could do. In Oslo, I learned that a newly built ship, the *Sagafjord,* was about to make its maiden voyage from Oslo to New York. I booked passage on the ship and had an idea that I might write a Profile of the trip for *The New Yorker.* While wandering around the *Sagafjord,* I looked in on a lounge where a couple of dozen passengers were enthusiastically singing "Get Me to the Church on Time," to the accompaniment of the Harald Jensen Kvartet. Among the singers, I found Gerd Nyquist, who was known as the Agatha Christie of Scandinavia. Gerd had been a leader in the Norwegian underground. The German SS came to her house to arrest her, but she scooped up her two small boys and fled out a back window and escaped to Sweden. I told Gerd and her husband, Arild, about my mission to Norway. Of course, they said, they would see what they could do to help me when the baby was born.

Back in New York, I found a lawyer who told me what to do about immigration procedures. Bill and Jerry Salinger and my gynecologist and my internist and his wife went in a merry band to the Norwegian Consulate and testified about my worthiness to be a mother. Papers and more papers were filled out and signed. The baby was born. A boy. He weighed five and a half pounds. He was eighteen inches long. (As I write this, he weighs 175 pounds and is six feet two inches long.) The nurses in the hospital where he was born were fighting with each other for the privilege of holding him. The Norwegian Parliament met in Oslo to debate the issue of whether this baby should be given to me. The Norwegian social worker spoke for me. Agnes Haug spoke for me. Gerd Nyquist spoke especially forcefully for me. The Parliament voted yes. I paid the baby's hospital bill of 184 kroner, about twenty-four dollars (socialized medicine). The baby was placed in my arms. (I don't know how it is for other adopters, but I never imagined him looking like anyone but himself.) Bill and I decided over the telephone to name him Erik, the "E" for my mother, Edna, the "K," for the Norwegian spelling.

I put Erik in a Scandinavian baby-carrying bed and flew with him to New York. As we were going through customs at the airport, I looked up to the place where friends and relatives were waiting. I took a picture that I treasure: Bill was standing there behind the glass wall, wearing his coat and his hat, and he was waving and crying. The three of us got into a taxi and went home and lived happily ever after. Erik was beautiful. His eyes were brown.

Erik's arrival on the scene set off a deluge of welcoming poems, to Erik from Bill, that continued for the rest of Bill's life.

Several women I know have told me that I provided a model for them by going out in 1966, unmarried, and adopting a baby. They used the word "brave" about me. The effect has been to make me feel like a bit of a fraud. I don't think I am brave. Without the support and full parental participation of Bill, I never, never would have been able to adopt and raise a child. Bill was with me at every turn along the way, helping with every decision—about Erik's pram (the biggest, heaviest, safest, costliest English job), his crib (we changed cribs three times before settling on the "prettiest"), his diapers (cloth), his first shoes (white), where to take his first step (our living room); worrying about every doctor's shot, every temperature over 98.6, every consideration about "the right school," every selection of a birthday present. My brother, Simeon, also was there for me and for Erik—celebrating holidays, building sandcastles on the beach, giving how-to-shave instructions, and so forth. Alone, I never could have coped with it—the uncertainties about every burp and grimace, the scares of the first illness, the worries about nutty old nannies, the nagging from outside parties about "When is he going to walk?" and "Why does he need to go to sleep with eight fire engines?," the choice of piano teachers, the choice of play

As we were going through customs at the airport, I looked up to the place where friends and relatives were waiting. I took a picture that I treasure. Bill was standing there behind the glass wall, wearing his heavy coat and his hat, and he was waving and crying.

When Bill and I decided to have a christening ceremony for the baby, Bill helped select the church and an actual fat lady who sang.

groups, the doubts about untrustworthy playmates and their untrustworthy parents, the problems of schools, the problems of summer camps, the answers to first questions, the answers to harder questions, five thousand apprehensions about all the lurking hostilities and dangers. I have unqualified esteem for women who can do it alone, but I am not one of them.

When Bill and I decided to have a christening ceremony for the baby, Bill helped select the church and an actual fat lady who sang. Because Erik was born "an unbaptized boy" in Norway, where state and church are one, Bill and I—both of us Jewish and both of us not formally religious—decided that he should not be deprived of this particular boon. Bill was convincingly adamant, much more than I was, about not making Erik Jewish. I was more intent on wanting him to have the christening he would have had automatically in Norway if he had remained there. So Bill and Jerry Salinger officially became Erik's godfathers. His godmother, Gerd Nyquist, came from Norway to attend the christening, along with my family and Jerry Salinger and Renata Adler and the filmmakers Ismail Merchant and James Ivory (they were interested at the time in *Vertical and Horizontal* as a possible movie) and Bill Shawn and others. Afterward we had a delightful party at the Carlyle, with Erik smiling and slurping on his bottle as he oversaw the festivities.

After I adopted Erik, I became aware of a change in me that had already taken place years before. I had been keeping the selfish writer in me on the back burner for a long time before I started looking for a baby. I simply felt confident that working could wait. I also understood, perhaps arrogantly, that what had been adding up in me was a storehouse that I could draw on in writing for the rest of my life. For now, there were long periods when I preferred to stay home and watch the baby. He was endlessly fascinating. I would often stay up half the night just watching Erik sleep. Finally, I installed a playpen and a hot plate in my office, and Bill would take us both down in a taxi every morning, and we would all go to work. (That arrangement, too, "broke new ground," I was told.)

I started telling Erik when he was two months old about Bill and our life together. All along the line, I told him everything, openly and truthfully. I always thought of a quote from J. D. Salinger's story "Raise High the Roof-Beam, Carpenters"—"They have ears. They can hear." Bill and I together, perhaps because of my childhood experience with my baby brother, Teddy, would repeatedly get Erik to mimic the cadence of "Erik." In fact, we did it so much that four-month-old Erik, as soon as he saw Bill, would sound out "Erik" on his own. Just before Erik started to crawl, the neighbor living next door to us on the twelfth floor moved out, and I took that apartment as well. We had a large hole chopped in the wall between apartments, and now Erik had a room of his own. Bill, Erik, and I continued going together to *The New Yorker* office, where Erik played, cooed, napped, and basked in the demonstrative attentions of the staff people, including William Maxwell, the fiction editor, who regularly kidnapped the baby and had him snooze on his office sofa. I worked. Bill worked. Then the three of us went home together. Bill was tender and loving and surprisingly eager to cuddle the baby. He played with the baby and read *The New Yorker* to him. I made supper. We ate. Erik went to sleep. Bill would go home and return in time to watch the late news.

Bill spent hours with Erik, playing the piano for him, reading to him, teaching him how to snare a baseball in a glove, getting beaten in checkers. When Erik was in grade school, Bill sat through a share of those excruciatingly long "teacher-parent conferences about your child." We started taking him to restaurants with us when he was a baby, and he became accustomed to eating our kind of food. He refused to eat peanut-butter-and-jelly sandwiches and still won't touch the

Bill spent hours with Erik, playing the piano for him, reading to him, teaching him how to snare a baseball in a glove, getting beaten in checkers.

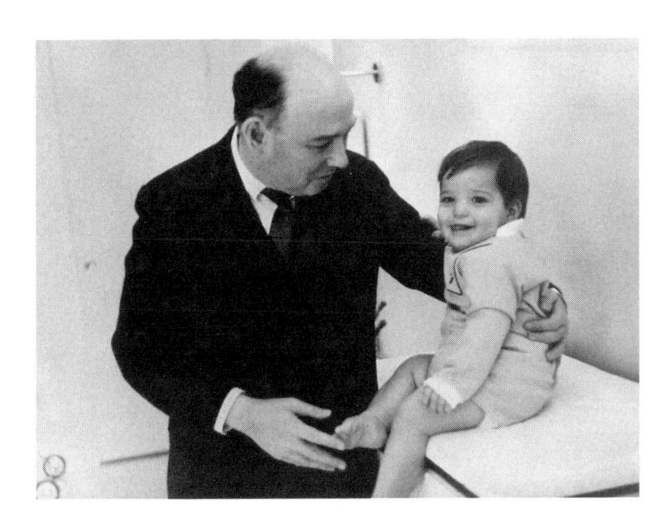

Bill was tender and loving and surprisingly eager to cuddle the baby.

stuff. Bill and I took Erik along with us—at first in his carrying bag, then in the stroller, and, from the age of two, on his own feet—just about wherever we went. He listened to everything we talked about—personal feelings or problems, news events, *The New Yorker,* office doings and aggravations, writing we loved, writing we disliked. Usually, we took along a friend of Erik's, and the friend listened in on everything, too. One of our daily hangouts was P. J. Clarke's, an oldtime favorite newspapermen's saloon, which served great hamburgers and home fries, and there, while eating, our foursome would regularly play the game I Spy. When Erik started tennis, Bill would accompany us on Saturdays to the Central Park courts to watch us play (a couple of times, he actually took a racquet in hand and demonstrated his somewhat rusty forehand). Afterward, we would take the tennis pro's two kids and make the usual beeline to Clarke's.

Erik never asked us the question "Why don't I have a daddy?" He grew up assuming that everybody had a "Bill" around. When he first heard the word "dad," he thought it was a proper name. Before Erik, we were a self-contained couple. Now we were a self-contained trio. And I couldn't resist using Erik as a subject, from time to time, in writing little pieces for "The Talk of the Town"—for example, "Writer" (April 14, 1973).

We're identifying strongly this week with a seven-year-old boy named Erik, who came home from school in high spirits one afternoon and told his mother he had been writing a story in class.

"Do you want to hear what my story is about?" Erik asked his mother.

"Sure," she said.

" 'Once upon a time, there was a dog, and the dog was very lonely, because he had no master' is the way my story starts," Erik said. " 'So this dog looked all over for somebody to be his

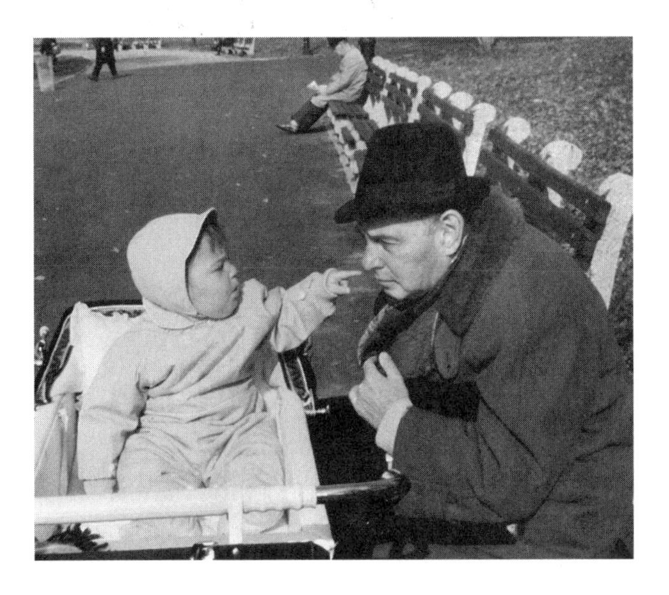

I started telling Erik when he was two months old about Bill and our life together. All along the line I told him everything, openly and truthfully.

Erik liked being held by Jerry Salinger.

master, and he couldn't find anybody to take him home. The dog was very sad, and, finally, one day he found a boy who became the dog's master. The boy played with the dog, but he hit the dog, so the dog decided not to let the boy be his master. The dog went all over the world, and finally, in New York City, he found a boy who took him home and played with him and didn't hit him, and ran around with him, and played tennis with him, and the dog lived with this boy as his master, and they were very happy living together forever after,' and that's the story I'm writing."

"I like the story," Erik's mother said. "I'd like to read it."

"I wrote part of the story today," Erik said. "I wrote 'Once.' "

When Erik was about eight, I woke up to the fact that he wasn't officially a United States citizen, so we set about filling out the usual forms and giving him a copy of the Pledge of Allegiance. When he was called for his interview at the offices of the Immigration and Naturalization Services, I took him there. To my astonishment, as we sat in the waiting room, an official approached us, brusquely took Erik by the arm, and, telling me firmly to sit down, announced that he was going to see Erik "alone." Erik looked puzzled. I was alarmed, watching my child being lugged off without me to the "interview." Fifteen minutes later, the official returned and, saying nothing and looking grim, deposited a pale-looking Erik in the chair alongside me.

"What did he say to you?" I asked my son, who seemed terribly frightened and, for a while, unable to speak. I hugged him. "What did he do? What did he say?" I asked again.

Finally, Erik said, in a low, little voice, "He said to me, 'Are you a Communist?' "

I suppressed my tremulous rage and gave Erik another hug. "Did you say no or what? What did you tell the man?" I asked.

"I told him I was a Norwegian at first, but now I'm going to vote," Erik said.

When we told Bill about the "interview," he gasped and gave Erik his own hug.

Bill and I did the usual "What if?" talk about the future: What if he should die? What if I were unable to care for Erik? What if Erik were bereft of a responsible adult? What if I needed financial help? If anything like that happened, Bill said with complete confidence, his son Wallace would be the person we should go to. He said that Wallace was the best person he knew, the most decent, the kindest, the most responsible; he knew that we could always count on Wallace. But at that point, we couldn't really believe that such emergencies might arise. We were in love, and apparently, when you're in love, you think you really *are* going to live forever.

All along the line, Bill and I shared the good news and the bad news of our families. We tried to familiarize each other with family milestones and family myths. When, in September 1955, during the intermission of a Royal Ballet performance we were attending, I made a telephone call to my brother, Simeon, and learned that his wife, Estelle, had just given birth to nonidentical twin girls—an unexpected doubling—Bill and I celebrated with caviar and champagne and gave the new parents our suggestions for the babies' names (and approval of their choices: Nancy and Louise). Bill grieved with me over the death of his brother Mike's wife. He laughed with me over his brother Harold's latest cutting-up on his violin. Bill told me about the relatives he loved. His favorite, Aunt Flora, was a very beautiful and romantic figure—Bill was struck with the way she held her ivory fan. We laughed about his cousin Belle, with whom he had once uncomfortably felt he was in love. Belle and her husband (an eminent proctologist) lived in a beautiful (and intimidating) New York apartment, where they gave very elegant and prestigious dinner parties to which Bill was invited only once. We went searching in shops for a fan like Flora's fans, and when we found one, Bill gave it to me.

When his sister's son, Billy, visited New York from Toronto, we took him to lunch at the Algonquin. When Bill's brother Mike, who had written the jingle for Wrigley's Doublemint Gum ("Double your pleasure, double your fun"), came from Chicago, Bill asked me to join them for lunch. One day his late brother's son, Nelson, Jr., visited the office, and Bill left him with me for a long talk about photography. Bill and I took my twin six-year-old nieces, Nancy and Louise Ross, ice-skating in Central Park and to a neighborhood delicatessen for memorable tongue sandwiches. That's the way it went. When my sister, Helen, died, Cecille graciously let me know, via Bill, that she was sorry.

The conventional routine of "lunch" with writers and artists bothered Bill, but he gamely followed it because, he would say, "it makes them feel better." The only such lunches he really enjoyed were those with S. N. Behrman, the comic playwright and screenplay writer (of some of the Marx Brothers movies, among others). Mr. Behrman, who suffered from depression, Bill told me, and couldn't bear to be alone, was married to the violinist Jascha Heifetz's sister, but they rarely went out together. Mr. Behrman wrote some unusual Profiles for the magazine, and both men looked forward to their encounters. They always took place at the Plaza. Bill would return to the office from a Behrman lunch happy and smiling, his face flushed. "He always makes me laugh!" Bill would say, laughing again at the recollection. One day after a Behrman lunch he burst into my office. "He told me a story about Billy Wilder, the movie director," Bill said, trying to contain himself. "It seems that Billy Wilder has amassed a very, very expensive art collection. Degas. Matisses. Van Goghs. Renoirs. A lot of Impressionists. And

Billy Wilder was telling Mr. Behrman about how all these guests were coming to his house only to see his art collection and to talk about his art collection. And nobody was talking about Billy Wilder's movies. So Billy Wilder was very cranky, because he felt he was being upstaged by his damn art collection. And besides, Billy Wilder said, every artist represented in his collection was dead, and all that the damn art collection did was to remind him of his own death!" Bill laughed and went on: "Mr. Behrman said he told Billy Wilder that he was glad that he had been spared the misfortune of having an art collection!" Bill laughed some more. It was a grand sight. I said I wished we had Sam Behrman hanging around all the time.

In mid-December one year, Mr. Behrman was ill. I sent him some Greenberg rolls and cakes to cheer him up, along with a little note saying I hoped he'd find them interesting. He replied with one of his inimitable S. N. Behrman letters:

Dear Lillian,

I will make the considered statement that in all this wide land there is no one with the acute scent for interesting breads and cakes that you have. I will go farther. I will say that were it not for your congenital shyness and the general lack of confidence that I feel in you, you might easily develop a similar infallibility in the discovery of interesting meats, eggs, lamb chops, cauliflowers—in fact over the whole vast field of nutrition. I do wish you would branch out and this, I confess, not merely because of my impulse to encourage the young. As I age, as the demand for me from the fields of gold out West wanes, as, to be blunt, the economic horizon narrows, a widening of your talents and an active pursuit of them, would decrease my dependence and concern for my old age.

Shawn arrived here hard upon the arrival of the interesting cake. We had it. Shawn said: "No one sends me interesting cake." It was pitiful.

The other night I couldn't sleep. I got up and cut myself a piece. It's great with milk. It's great any time and without anything.

Please expand!

Love and Thanks,
Sam

When Bill's sons were still small, he told me, he would try to play the piano with them, with Wallace on the violin and Allen on drums. He said that he felt they knew about us when they were teenagers, or even younger, because of his absences from their home. But "working" was always given as the answer to their questions about those absences. One evening, when he was calling me from home, he got caught up in talking and laughing about one of my "Vertical and Horizontal" stories. "It's so *funny*," Bill was saying, through his laughter. He was interrupted at that moment by Wallace, who wanted to know why his father was laughing. Bill explained that he was "telling Lillian Ross about a funny scene in her story." Bill didn't feel free to speak fully about Erik and me to his children until years later, but he was always truthful in answering their questions involving my name. He didn't know how to do otherwise. When his nephew Fred, son of Cecille's sister, came to visit them, Bill had him come to meet me. "Maybe you can explain Fred to me," Bill said wistfully. "He knows how to roll around with Wallace and Allen on the floor in what is called 'horseplay.' "

Bill had me come to hear Wallace's graduation speech at his elementary school. He had me come, on May 10, 1962, to a concert in which Allen played one of his compositions, a set of variations for piano and orchestra entitled "Older Brother." He told me how Wallace had packed his violin, his typewriter, and an enormous box of books to take with him to a summer sports camp. He shared reports about Allen's early music compositions and his conducting as a child at a music camp. He listened repeatedly to Allen's later, "modern" compositions until he began to understand them. They were intriguing, he explained, but they were "beyond" him. "Which means," he would say, with a smile, "they're too good." He had me read an extraordinary piece Wallace wrote about a postmaster in India when he was there on a Fulbright scholarship after college. The piece was a knockout, and I said so, adding that Wallace should be writing for *The New Yorker.* Bill looked delighted. I agonized with Bill when Wallace, very ill in some mountainous region near India, had not communicated with his parents for weeks. I measured crazy dangers with Bill repeatedly every time Wallace went off to places like El Salvador (during its war in the 1980s), to Mexico, to the Dominican Republic. I heard about this girlfriend and that girlfriend of both sons, and the meetings of parents with parents, and I heard about Allen's romance with and marriage to the writer Jamaica Kincaid.

Bill started telling me about Wallace in my first years at the magazine—about his remarkable intelligence as a baby, when Bill kept a list of the words in what became a highly unusual baby vocabulary; about Wallace's volatility at the age of seven, which worried Bill; about his kindness and generosity to a troubled girl in high school; about his unusual roommates at Harvard; about his acceptance of the Fulbright award and immediate departure from home; about his courage in finding his own way to conquer his asthma; about his stint as a Latin teacher and dramatic coach at the Day School; about his attempts to write plays and his success, without any help from Bill, in getting the Public Theater to produce his first play, *Our Late Night.* Bill told me his worries about what Wallace ate (including his appetite for garlic, which Bill hated). Bill would tell me how deeply he respected Wallace's independence. He told me of his affection for Wallace's companion, the writer Deborah Eisenberg, and about the way they made their living—Wallace working in a Xerox copying shop and Debbie working as a waitress—while they tried to write. He brought me up to date over the years about Debbie's very affecting short stories, which he admired enormously and published; about Wallace's big success with the movie *My Dinner with André,* which he co-wrote and acted in; about Wallace's fascination with Los Angeles (especially the legendary, Hollywood hotel Chateau Marmont) and his funny and agreeable adventures in the movie business. Bill told me about Allen's application to music schools, about his composing, about his studies in Paris with Nadia Boulanger, about a musical play he wrote, with a scene featuring a man eating what Bill told me was *his* breakfast. He told me how Wallace and Allen moved out on the same day and established themselves in their own apartments. He told me about Allen and Jamaica's decision to make their home in Bennington, Vermont, where Allen would teach music. As Bill continued to tell me about Wallace and Allen, there was an inevitable building up in me of a reservoir of feeling and memory that led me to feel close to them. I knew so much about them, and when I saw them, I was always vaguely surprised that *they* didn't know that.

When Bill was with his family, I felt no resentment, no envy. I never felt "left out." I might wonder from time to time why I *didn't* long to be with them. I had a wholly natural affection for all of them that felt right, that felt normal. But they were not part of my life with Bill, and it was my life with Bill, I realized, that was giving me everything I wanted, everything I needed. I never felt deprived. When the Norwegians Agnes Haug and her husband, Bjørn, came to New York, Bill and I took them to the Algonquin for a festive lunch. Gerd Nyquist, Erik's godmother, would visit us often, and Bill always insisted on gallant dining at La Caravelle and celebratory entertainments. Bill and I found in Erik the classic pleasures of parenthood and rejoiced in every forward step he took in life. When Erik was at Harvard, he let us see an imitation of a seventeenth-century poem he had been assigned to write for an English literature class with Professor William Alfred. The poem was entitled—thrillingly, to us—"To Mom." ("Ye all who stand and listen to my voice/Will find it hard to stand and not rejoice/About the one who truly must have praise;/Cannot but help to let their voices raise...") Bill and I always spoke on the telephone if we were apart, to say good night or to exchange thoughts. I might miss him, but I was never lonely. In fact, I enjoyed the respites of being alone, with my own thoughts and feelings, with my work, with Erik, with tennis, with my gratifying runs around the Central Park Reservoir.

I was always free to take off whenever I felt like it. And take off I did, frequently, especially after Erik came on board. Disney World was one of our favorite vacation places—best hotels, best tennis, best swimming, best sailing, best Americana, and best amusement park high jinks—where we didn't have to talk to anybody unless we felt like it. One August, I took off for Aspen, Colorado, where my clarinet teacher, Reginald Kell, was spending the summer teaching. I took clarinet lessons, rode a horse, and talked every night on the telephone to Bill. Whenever Erik went with me on a trip, working or otherwise, we telephoned Bill every night to keep him informed of our adventures. I took Erik to Oslo several times to show him his "roots," and we traveled to Moscow when I wanted to have a look at my own. From Norway, I had to explain to Bill over the telephone that eight-year-old Erik, on the Nyquists' schooner in a fjord, was jumping overboard with the Nyquists' grandchildren and swimming under the boat to come up on the other side, because it was a very *Norwegian* thing to do. (Bill was appalled.) When I was in Moscow, we had some highly nervous consultations. The time I had chosen to look at my Russian roots—the early summer of 1968—was not exactly propitious; it turned out to be on the eve of the Soviet invasion of Czechoslovakia. I went with

Erik from Moscow to Peredelkino by car to visit Kornei Chukovsky, the poet, author of children's stories, and translator of Walt Whitman. Such trips by foreigners were then illegal. Chukovsky fed us borscht, caviar, and blinis, but he himself lapped up the entire emergency supply of two-year-old Erik's food I had brought from the United States—Beechnut baby food jars of creamed chicken, sweet potatoes, and cherry custard. The KGB followed us to Peredelkino, spied on our activities, including our feastings, and threatened me for having broken the law. (Bill was appalled.)

When Erik was twelve, François Truffaut invited me to come to Paris in June, when school let out, to watch him shoot *Love on the Run* (*L'amour en fuite*) and to appear in a scene of passengers in a dining car on a train. So we took a celebratory trip to Paris. This time Erik joined me in retracing the paths and haunts I had visited for Bill twenty-four years before. We went to see—and to photograph for Bill again—the little hotel at 44 rue Jacob, the one with the fountain in the courtyard. I told Erik that it used to be called the Hôtel Jacob, and that now it was called the Hôtel d'Angleterre. We went to the Café aux Deux Magots, and we sat in the Jardin des Plantes. I told Erik about walking in the "violet light of the Tuileries" and how it felt when Bill told me that he and I "walked there together holding hands and giving each other everything good that we have it in our power to give." Then Erik and I went to the restaurant that was called La Cloche when Bill played there, in the bar downstairs, on the piano in the back room. The little restaurant, now called La Petite Chaise, still had wonderful food. We went downstairs, but the area was still a storeroom, and there still was no piano in the back room. But the food in the restaurant was tops, and we ate supper there every night for a week—Quenelles de Brochet à l'Armoricaine, Canard à l'Orange, Filet au Poivre, and Crêpes Suzette. Over the telephone, when we described it all to Bill, he again said we'd "woven together some bright and faded threads of time."

In Truffaut's movie, Erik and I enjoyed "acting" (we just sat at the table and pretended to eat) with Jean-Pierre Léaud and Marie-France Pisier. One evening, Truffaut invited us to have real food in his home. He showed us his extensive collection of toy and model statuettes and paintings of the Eiffel Tower and his stupendous view of the real one from his apartment window. Then he gave Erik several books from his collection about mystery and monster movies. We went to London (feeding pelicans and swans in St. James's Park, riding the double-deckers, walking back and forth across Westminster Bridge, taking in the fossil galleries in the British Museum, visiting the Science Museum, buying Erik a Harrods raincoat). We came home on the Concorde ($833 one way in 1977). I wrote a Talk story, "Quick," about it, quoting Erik: "The nose down creates a drag and allows the pilots to have a better view of the runway. We'll be landing like any other plane but at a greater angle to the landing strip. There are no flaps on the Concorde wings to slow the plane down while landing, so the entire body of the aircraft acts as a flap." In 1988, to celebrate Erik's graduation from college, we went again to Paris. Erik remembered La Petite Chaise. We ate there every night for a week.

Bill was always with me when I needed him or wanted him. His voice was the first voice I heard when I came out of the anesthesia after the operation. "I am here, I am here," he was saying. Gradually, I had come to appreciate the daily pleasures and joys and fulfillments of our relationship. There were still those mornings when he picked me up in a taxi to go to work when his face revealed the remonstrance, accusations, and guilt he had brought with him from his home. Even then, I could feel no bitterness, only a vague sadness at our three-way predicament. Flagellation, self- or otherwise, was pointless and destructive.

As human creatures, we crawl along and do the best we can as we go. When Bill worried about his wife or talked about being "there but not there," I worried with him. But I could not disappear. That I could not do. And that would not have changed basic problems that had nothing to do with me. Cecille was always courteous and helpful to me in all the scheduling matters that would come up in our lives. In later years, when Bill was in the hospital—with the dubious "heart attack," the hernia operations, the cataract operations—Cecille would telephone me promptly to report the news of the outcomes. We would arrange our visiting hours so that we would avoid encounters. If I needed to make a change in our routines, or if Bill and I wanted to do something special with Erik, we made arrangements and rearrangements among the three of us. I never lost sight of what was most important to me—the daily living.

I never was made to feel that anyone around me was being judgmental about what I was doing with Bill. A few acquaintances, attached to each other legally, with some elementary knowledge of us as a couple, were curious. Some of them had a need to compare our relationship with their legitimate ones, which usually seemed to me to be badly in need of repair. The fact is that no husband or father I've ever known gave more than Bill gave to me and to Erik. Bill observed with wonder that he had spent weekday and weekend time with Erik from his babyhood until he was in his twenties. Our favorite restaurant, La Caravelle, would see as much of Erik as they saw of Bill and me. The structure of my life with Bill, even within the perimeters, enclosed more solidity, more purpose, more satisfaction, and even more social responsibility than most conventional arrangements. He told me he was determined to give me "everything," and he tried to do exactly that. Not once did I feel that I was making some kind of noble "sacrifice" for him. It gave me enormous pleasure when he let me know, daily, that he did, indeed, exist. Also, I would think, Who was it decreed that a man and a woman in love with each other must be with each other at all times? Bill often would say to me that we were together more than most married couples. That, too, I knew, was a fact. He would say that the nature of our union was untouchable, unreachable, unimpeachable. Another fact.

"Our time together defied death," Bill would say. In a mystical way, even that became a fact.

Bill observed family occasions with his sons as well as with Mary and, later, with his two grandchildren. His life with Cecille continued, outside of our own. Thanksgiving, from year to year, was a kind of annual marker for the continuity of that life. Every year, Bill would give me a report on the dinner and its regulars, including, in our early years, his uncle Sam, a former baseball player and actor. Erik and I never felt deprived of Thanksgiving. Bill observed all the holidays with Erik and me on our own designated festive days. Christmas Eve always belonged to us. We usually went to see *The Nutcracker* at Lincoln Center, and then we would go to La Caravelle for dinner. Every New Year's Eve, over our forty years together, if we were apart, I would have a telephone call from Bill at precisely twelve midnight. All logistical matters were minor or irrelevant; nothing really mattered except our day-to-day life. I marveled at the startling nature of this fact: nothing else really *mattered.*

In the mid 1970s, and especially in the early 1980s when Erik was in boarding school, I found that I was able to do more writing—Talk stories and Profiles, including those of Francis Ford Coppola and Akira Kurosawa. I wrote a memoir about Charlie Chaplin, who died in 1977 ("Moments with Chaplin"). I started working on a Profile of François Truffaut, about whom I had written several Talk stories, beginning with one, in 1960, when he came over here from Paris to introduce his film *The 400 Blows.* One summer, while Erik was in a tennis camp, I met Truffaut in Beverly Hills. He came to the Beverly Hills Hotel from Paris once or twice a year for the express purpose of daily visiting his idol and friend, Jean Renoir, who, among other films, had directed, and played in, the classic 1939 film *Rules of the Game.* (Bill took me to see that film, one he was inordinately and emotionally partial to, every time he could find a theatre playing it, no matter how small or seedy or out-of-the way.)

Truffaut worshiped all of Renoir's work. Truffaut would stay at the Beverly Hills Hotel for ten days. He never put on a bathing suit. He never went into a swimming pool. He never went to the beach. He never tried to see anyone but Renoir. Every day, Truffaut would get up early in the morning and stay in his hotel room, watching television, until it was time to go out to see Renoir. He would rent a convertible and drive it only to visit Renoir. On every visit, they would watch a different movie they both liked. One afternoon Truffaut took me along, driving against a glaring sun in the rented convertible, to Renoir's house in Beverly Hills. We found Renoir—at that time near the end of his life—in a wheelchair. His wife fussed over him and spread a blanket over his lap. Burgess Meredith, another guest, had written, produced, and starred in Jean Renoir's 1946 movie *Diary of a Chambermaid,* which had also starred Paulette Goddard, Meredith's wife at that time. Meredith now arrived—exuberant, cheerful, and raspy-voiced—and asked what movie we were going to see. Truffaut said solemnly, in English, "*Ride the Pink Horse.*"

"Ah. With Robert Montgomery," Meredith said. "Directed by Bob Montgomery himself. Way back in 1947."

He exchanged triumphant looks with Truffaut and Renoir, who exchanged solemn looks with each other. "A good film," Truffaut said. "A very good *film-noir.*"

"A very good film," Renoir said.

A projectionist arrived and quickly and silently set up a sixteen-millimeter film projector and a portable screen. The room was darkened. From the beginning to the end of the movie, Truffaut and Renoir, both still solemn, demonstrated that they knew the film by heart. Jointly, they anticipated every shot, murmuring to each other about a camera angle, about a bit of lighting, about a move by an actor, about each turn of the plot. They seemed to float in a knowledgeable and empathetic world that was theirs and theirs alone. Burgess Meredith was like a cheerful Greek chorus. At the end of the movie, everybody shook hands all around.

"*À demain,*" Truffaut said to Renoir.

"*À demain,*" said Renoir.

Then Truffaut went out with me into the still-glaring sunlight, got into his rented car, returned to his room at the Beverly Hills Hotel, ordered a peanut-butter-on-white-bread sandwich and a Coke from room service, and watched television until three in the morning.

Later, over the telephone, I told Bill about my afternoon. I told him that because of the way I felt, I might not be able to write about it.

"Yes," he said, hoarsely. "I love you."

"I love you," I said.

I liked writing about movie directors I admired, and I welcomed the opportunity to catch up with some I had profiled earlier. I always got a big kick out of finding a fresh story in Federico ("Call me Freddy") Fellini, about whom I had written a Profile in 1965. The occasion then was my first visit to Italy, and I was on the telephone constantly with Bill, regaling him with accounts of all the fun I was having with Fellini—watching him at work at his film studio, visiting an old church, accompanying him to his Fregene beach home for lunch with him and his wife, the actress Giulietta Masina, taking a nap in a darkened room after lunch because Fellini said, "Now we go to sleep." Bill's hunger to be carefree in Rome or wherever was endless, and he would hang on every detail of my adventures. I loved telling him about them, and then it would double the pleasure (and the laughter) to give him my written reports.

I wrote several stories about Fellini, the last one in 1985, when he telephoned and said he was coming to New York. He arrived—with his wife, Giulietta, with Marcello Mastroianni, and with the actress Anouk Aimée—to be honored by Lincoln Center's Film Society. Fellini invited me, and also Erik, to go with him and his gang for a Sunday afternoon at the Darien, Connecticut, country home of Dorothy Cullman, the Film Society's chairman. It was the first time Fellini et al. had ever been to what they all pronounced "Conneckticut." I wrote the story, as usual, with Bill in mind, so that he might participate in all of it—their asking if "Grant's Tomb" was "Cary's"; Mastroianni's wanting to know why the Colonial houses were built of wood instead of, as in Italy, stone; their puzzled reaction to the Cullmans' obligatory tour of their old house and to the description of its renovations, remodeling, and decoration; their appreciative consumption of crabmeat and pâté appetizers; and their gratitude to Erik, the only one of the bunch to take the obligatory swim in the pool. And Bill gave me what I'd always sought over the years—his laughter.

Erik and I were friendly with Wallace and Allen Shawn whenever we would see them. After Allen married the writer Jamaica Kincaid, they made overtures of friendship. We exchanged small Christmas gifts. I gave them a framed photograph I had taken of Bill. Then they invited me over to their small, cozy apartment downtown. Bill had never been to their apartment (or to Wallace's) because of his claustrophobia. When I asked him if he had any objections to my visiting Allen and Jamaica, he said he'd be pleased. So I went, and it was a sweet and friendly visit. We talked about Erik, and they said that they felt he was their brother. I told Bill about the visit, and he was very moved.

Jamaica came to Erik's high school graduation, and we were glad to have her there. She was well along in her pregnancy with her daughter, Bill's first grandchild, Annie. On the day of the baby's birth, I was happy to accept Jamaica's invitation to come to the hospital as First Visitor and to give a glowing report to Bill that the baby was lifting her head and looking things over in her raring-to-go first hours.

On Erik's fifth birthday, Bill gave him a puppy, a small, apricot-colored miniature poodle. My brother, Simeon, made a short film of Bill presenting Erik with the puppy. Erik named her Goldie. Erik now guarded *his* puppies with his life. She grew up and had two litters of apricot-colored poodles in our apartment. The third litter, the product of a liaison with a black toy, brought forth two all-black poodles. We named them Romulus and Remus, and they went to live with Erik's uncle Simeon in the country. (When Erik went away to high school and to college, I found myself bringing Goldie to the *New Yorker* office with me.) Bill gave me a the Leica Reflex camera, and we took hundreds of photographs of ourselves in our happy life. They may not have been Norman Rockwell pictures, but they came close—close enough, at any rate—to the scenes on the covers of the *Collier's Weekly* magazines I sold as a child.

Erik went to a traditional private school in the neighborhood, where he learned to speak and write grammatically. Bill heroically attended interminable plays and concerts and parents' meetings. Other children would question Erik about Bill, and they would tell him about their family life, but Erik always had the feeling—possibly soaked up from Bill and from me—that his situation was not only fine but preferable to theirs. He put up with some jabs from peers and parents, and occasionally his feelings may have been hurt, but he always refused to respond to violence with violence. From Bill, he had learned to respond to hostility by offering good will and kindness. Nonetheless, when Erik was about six or seven,

My friendship with John Huston and his family continued for a good thirty-five years after I initially wrote about him in my book *Picture.* Here he holds Erik.

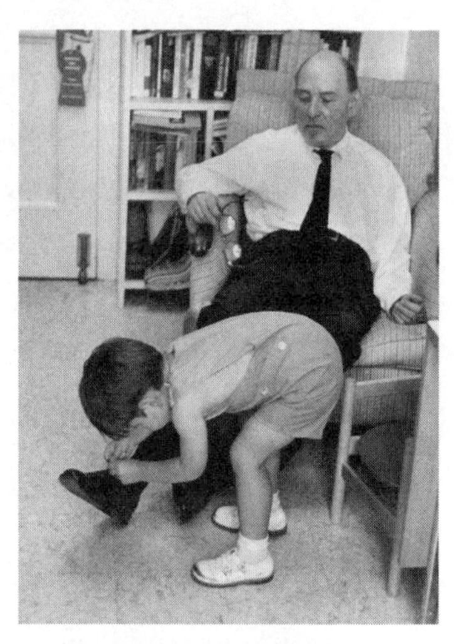

Erik would have lunch with us in my office and kid around with Bill.

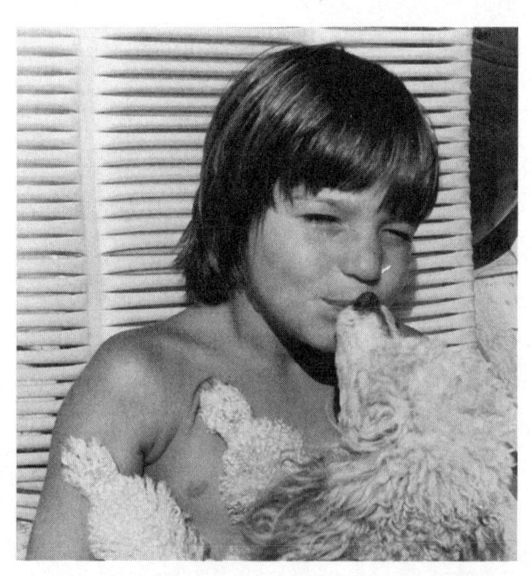

On Erik's fifth birthday, Bill presented him with an apricot-colored miniature poodle. Erik named her Goldie.

with the emphasis all around me on "family values," I had some lingering doubts about whether I was fully exposing Erik to the right values. In my overeagerness to show him some role-model family life, we participated, occasionally with Bill, in some conventional families' family activities. The families were very kind and generous to us, and for the first time in my life, I had some insight into what Tolstoy meant when he began *Anna Karenina* by writing "Happy families are all alike. Every unhappy family is unhappy in its own way." So Erik, Bill, and I were happy to conclude that our family pattern was excellent and essentially like those of the happy traditional families.

My friendships with my colleagues at the magazine continued. We did a lot of bike riding. Bill and I had bought Huffy bicycles (Bill had yearned for a Huffy, just as he had for a Triumph), and we would go out bike riding in Central Park on them, with Erik sitting in a baby seat behind me. We installed a baby seat on Bill's bike, too. Bill lent his bike to friends. The most frequent borrower was the fiction writer and film critic Penelope Gilliatt, whose young daughter, Nolan Osborne, was about Erik's age. Another biker on Bill's Huffy was Renata Adler, *sans* child. (Some years later, she adopted a little boy and, surprisingly, gave me credit for being her "role model.")

When Erik started sixth grade in school, I was giving more and more attention to my writing. With Erik, Bill and I continued to grow closer and closer, and I found myself becoming more and more sympathetic to the needs of his routine with Cecille. If she were laid low by the flu, for instance, I would be the one to insist on canceling our dinner plans so that he could go to her.

I didn't feel any surge of wishing to be with Cecille or to bring her into my life with Erik and Bill. But I did experience a growing feeling of friendliness toward her, as well as an acceptance of the part of Bill's life that she, and she alone, had shared. I had long since come to terms with the impossibility

Penelope Gilliatt, the film critic and fiction writer, would bring her daughter, Nolan Osborne, to play with Erik, and I would take the kids to the Carousel in Central Park.

of wiping out history. I also found myself wondering why I couldn't feel that I had anything in common with Cecille. I supposed that perhaps she felt that she didn't have anything in common with me. These were strange realizations for me. After all, we had, supposedly, shared the same man. Or had we?

CHAPTER 10

COLLABORATORS

In the early 1980s, Warren Buffet, together with his business partner, Charles Munger, contacted Bill and told him that they were interested in buying *The New Yorker* in order to protect it from a possible purchaser who might not feel the way they did about the magazine. There was discussion back and forth, during which Bill asked them whether, if they purchased *The New Yorker,* there would be a place in the management of it for Peter Fleischmann, the current owner. Their answer was no. In that case, Bill responded, as much as he would like having them, he could not support them. So they went away. And Bill never told Peter Fleischmann about their discussion. McGeorge Bundy, then president of the Ford Foundation, also wrote directly to Bill expressing concern about a possible change in the magazine's business control and offered to help Bill look into ways of calling in support via the Ford Foundation for protecting the independence of *The New Yorker*'s journalistic voice. Bill assured Bundy he knew of no impending change in the financial control of the magazine.

During this period, Bill knew and agonized over many of the problems besetting the business office at the magazine—Peter Fleischmann's illnesses, some self-aggrandizing individuals' actions. Bill was not a sophisticated businessman, but he could see, and he told me, that the business leadership should have been stronger. "But we're lucky," he said. "The magazine is still making a profit. The readers are loyal. The magazine is not the perfect magazine I would wish it to be, but it's still great." Moreover, he felt he had to abide by the traditional separation between the editorial and the business sides of the magazine. He could not bring himself to turn his back on Peter Fleischmann. He regretted having sent Warren Buffet away, but he remained loyal to the end to the business people already in his life.

When Peter Fleischmann decided to sell his controlling interest in *The New Yorker* to S. I. Newhouse, Jr., in 1985, it was a fait accompli by the time Bill and the editorial staff understood what was happening. Years earlier, Bill had divested himself of many shares of stock to avoid even a hint of "conflict of interest," so with the sale, Bill got nothing. He would have made $10 million, he told me, if he had held on to his stock. (He had bought some stock as gifts for Wallace and for Allen and Jamaica. At that time he asked me if I wanted him to buy some stock for me, and I said—impractically and perhaps, in retrospect, foolishly—no.)

Along with everybody else at *The New Yorker,* Bill Shawn was frightened and upset by conflicting and fuzzy rumors of the impending sale. I happened to be sitting in Bill's office when he heard the sale was definite. Too late, he was about to put through a telephone call to Warren Buffet to ask him if he could come to the magazine's rescue by bidding for it at a higher price. Before he could make the call, he had a call from Ted Clark, Peter Fleischmann's lawyer, informing him that the arrangements were irreversible. When the sale went through, for $168 million, Peter Fleischmann, as the largest stockholder, made a profit of $44 million. Bill was sorry that he did not make $10 million, but he was more upset by what he felt was Peter Fleischmann's betrayal of him and the staff. Also, he was afraid of what the new owner would do to the magazine. So he wrote an eloquent piece to be published in the "Notes and Comment" section of the magazine, to inform and reassure the readers about its editorial independence. The piece, he felt, would ensure the continuation of that independence:

> The business ownership of *The New Yorker* may change hands, but the idea of *The New Yorker*—the tradition of *The New Yorker*, the spirit of *The New Yorker*—has never been owned by anyone and never will be owned by anyone. It cannot be bought and sold....
>
> *The New Yorker* will continue to change, as it has changed through the years, but our basic principles and standards will remain exactly as they have been. With that knowledge, and with the assurances that we freely asked our prospective publishers to give us and that they freely gave, we are confident that we will preserve *The New Yorker*—not merely a magazine that bears its name but this magazine: *The New Yorker* itself.

A few skeptics at the magazine applauded the eloquence of the Comment, but they said that it was naive of Bill to assume that publishing these principles would ensure their survival. We would soon learn that there was no such insurance. What I would learn, though, was that naive and trusting people, no matter how much they might learn about insurance or no insurance, would go on being naive and trusting. And that, I would also learn, is not necessarily such a bad way to be.

After the stockholders voted and Advance Publications became the new owner—signed, sealed, and delivered—S. I. Newhouse invited Bill to come to his town house for breakfast. I took Bill there in a taxi, and as we drove up, we noticed

Mr. Newhouse standing at the second-floor window, peering from behind the drapes, like an anxious child waiting for a highly desirable playmate. Bill later told me that as soon as they sat down at the breakfast table, Bill knocked over his glass of orange juice, which led to the usual awkward semi-hysteria. This somehow created another basis for affection on Bill's part, an affection that he never abandoned. (Unlike most people, once Bill gave his loyalty or his affection to anyone, he never withdrew it, no matter how hurtful or disappointing the other person's actions toward him might be.) Shortly thereafter, Mr. Newhouse, elated, stated publicly that he had in his life been privileged to associate closely with the three most "charismatic" of men: his father, Samuel Newhouse, founder of the family business; his mentor, Alexander Liberman; and William Shawn.

At this point, Bill had reached the age of seventy-seven without any substantial change in his energy, in his mind, or in his charisma. Almost instantly, he became fond of S. I. Newhouse. He felt more of a connection to him than he had ever felt to the Fleischmanns, fond of them and loyal to them as he was. Why? My explanation may sound strange. One evening in the 1960s, Bill and I were having dinner at La Caravelle, and we saw Samuel I. Newhouse, Sr., the founder of the media empire, and his wife, Mitzi, with a couple of young boys, as they came in. It was clear to us that Newhouse felt very proud of, and at ease with what we decided was his family. Mitzi, looking flirtatious and confident, was wearing a black mini-skirted frock. The boys, in identical dark-blue suits, looked lost, awed, breathless, and excited to be there. Neither Bill nor I ever forgot that moment. I happen to believe in the power of such moments. And that is why I think that Bill felt a special connection with Si Newhouse.

Bill wanted to help Newhouse, and he thought he *could* help him. He wanted to protect him. He worried about the $168 million Newhouse had paid for the magazine. He felt guilty and somehow responsible for Newhouse's having paid too much, in Bill's opinion. Bill was determined to do everything in his power now to ensure a real future for *The New Yorker,* and he seemed to connect the security of the magazine's future with his own departure from it—just the opposite of wanting to "hang on." He wanted to clear the way for leaving it in other hands. Whose hands?

In the meantime, the magazine went on publishing wonderful writing, comic art, beautiful covers, everything still imbued with the spirit of William Shawn. And the readers, for the most part, were loyal to it. Yet Bill, more than anyone else at *The New Yorker,* was aware of its advertising problems and stayed awake nights worrying about its future.

I was still following the same daily routine with Bill, with my reporting, and with Goldie. And I was focused on Erik, in college, and starting to wonder about *his* future. He was handsome, six feet two inches tall, generous, compassionate, and very observant. He was the steady third party in my life with Bill. It was a life free of argument, bitterness, and noise. When I reached a point where I understood Bill, I accepted everything about him, including his weaknesses that might have been strengths. Somehow or other, I understood instinctively that to try to change him would be to destroy him.

Bill had been trying for years to find someone who might be trained as his successor. One candidate after another was considered. Bill was very fond of Jonathan Schell, whom he had known since childhood, and who had gone to school—Dalton, Putney, and Harvard—with his son Wallace. Bill had worked very closely with Schell on his writing at the magazine for the past twenty years. In 1967 and just out of college, Schell had gone on his own to Vietnam and had written a memorable piece, "The Village of Ben Suc," which Bill published. Thereafter, Bill worked with him on the many eloquent editorial Comments and then on *The Fate of the Earth.*

In 1978, Bill told Peter Fleischmann that the magazine's forceful editorials on the subjects of the Vietnam War and the

Nixon administration had added greatly to *The New Yorker*'s reputation for honesty and courage, and the magazine and the business had emerged from that tumultuous period "with honor and a new vigor." That led, Bill said, to winning the respect of a whole new generation of readers.

Bill saw a promising successor in Schell. Naively, he assumed that the key editorial colleagues and writers and artists at the magazine would see the same promise in Schell, and democratically, Bill tried to discuss his choice with his staff. Most of them agreed that Schell was a brilliant young man, a good writer, a good thinker, strong-minded, ethical, moral, devoted to Bill Shawn's principles and ideals. But they raged against Schell, saying he pretended he *was* Bill Shawn. None of what they said mattered. They raged because Schell could not make that essential connection with them. It was something they could feel. One time I asked Bill how he managed to tune in to the dozens and dozens of people he worked with, how he was able to make those connections. He said, almost gloomily, that he had never been aware of it; he had just done it. I asked him how important it was. "It's the most crucial element of all," he said. "Almost everything else can be learned."

One candidate after another was considered. Mr. Newhouse was pressuring Bill to have someone waiting in the wings, and the situation was becoming desperate, unnecessarily so, a lot of us thought, because Bill Shawn was still doing the job, and everybody was happy about that. On the other hand, Bill himself desperately wanted to be relieved of his responsibility. More and more, he spoke to me about what he called his "mistake" in having taken on the job in the first place, the "big mistake" of what he felt he had done with his life, the "ultimate cell" he was in. And yet he felt he could not abandon all the writers and artists who depended on him. The entrapment he had feared as a child had years ago become a nightmarish reality for him, but the daily needs over the years of all the creative people he worked with had always intruded and diffused the nightmare. Now Bill was feeling the urgency more keenly, and he was in a constant state of despair over his inability to find a solution to his problem.

In retrospect, it is somewhat puzzling to me that Bill Shawn never became a role model at *The New Yorker.* In effect, no writer, no artist, and no editor—with the exception of Jonathan Schell—wanted to be like him. When Jonathan Schell demonstrated that *he* wanted to be like him—and actually absorbed what he thought was Bill's persona—Bill's co-workers seemed to find this distasteful.

Meanwhile, Bill kept on talking to various people about the job. When Peter Fleischmann suggested a candidate, Bill told him that he had great affection, admiration, and respect for this candidate, but he disagreed about the choice. Nevertheless, Bill told him that if this candidate was given the job, he would cooperate in every possible way and teach him everything he knew. Then he went on to explain the kind of patience and devotion the job called for, and to spell out all of the responsibilities and complications his successor would have to take on. Mr. Fleischmann retreated and didn't go on with his candidate.

After a few more weeks of considering possible successors, Bill settled on a very solid, intelligent, perceptive fiction editor, Charles McGrath, who was extremely sensitive and knowledgeable and who understood, in his own quiet, non-flamboyant way, how to "tune in" to writers and artists. Bill started having a series of "tutorial lunches" with Charles McGrath, and both men were responding enthusiastically to each other.

Then Mr. Newhouse jumped the gun. He said he had found his own candidate: Robert Gottlieb, head of Knopf, the book publishing house also owned by Newhouse. Mr. Newhouse came to Bill's office and presented him with a copy of a news release he had already given to *The New York Times,* announcing Bill's "retirement."

More and more, he spoke to me about what he called his "mistake" in having taken on the job in the first place . . . and yet he felt he could not abandon all the writers and artists who depended on him.

Practically the entire staff—154 writers, artists, and editors—wrote a joint letter to Gottlieb, politely asking him not to come and pointing out that his appointment "had halted the orderly process, already well along, of providing the magazine with a new editor, Charles McGrath, from within its present ranks." Even J. D. Salinger signed the letter, though he complained that it wasn't "strong enough." Mr. Newhouse asked Bill to meet him at the Algonquin after work, and at the meeting he said to Bill, "Why did you let them send that letter?" Bill replied that he thought he should not interfere with what the staff wanted to do. So Mr. Newhouse, who had a car and driver, took Bill and me and Goldie home. In the car, Mr. Newhouse said that Gottlieb had "charisma," and then we talked about dogs. The next day, Gottlieb had his reply to the staff letter posted in the halls. In it, he said he had been given the job, and therefore he was coming.

The next several weeks were chaotic. In one way, Bill was relieved to have had the decision taken out of his hands. But he was very troubled about the way Robert Gottlieb had been thrust upon the staff and McGrath had been dropped. In retrospect, it seems clear to me, as well as to others, that it was the choice of Gottlieb that made for the resistance of the staff. Gottlieb had said publicly that he had three "ambitions" in life—to be head of Knopf; to be head of the New York City Ballet; and to be the editor-in-chief of *The New Yorker.* So he was realizing his third "ambition." To many of us "ambition" was not enough.

Bill was given about two months to get ready to leave. Many staff writers feverishly wrote stories they had been stalling around with for a long time. They wanted to be sure their pieces would be bought. Some writers finished writing two or three pieces. Bill purchased every one of them.

Bill made some lunch appointments with Gottlieb to explain to him how *The New Yorker* worked. He valiantly plunged ahead, trying to outline principles, procedures, who did what, what happened at the weekly art meeting, troubled writers, troubled artists, payments, contracts. Bill talked and talked and talked at these lunches.

"He doesn't seem to listen," Bill sadly told us back at the office. "He doesn't seem to want to hear anything."

I occupied myself with writing short pieces for "The Talk of the Town." The writers talked to one another about what they were going to do, now that Bill was being fired. Jonathan Schell quit immediately. "This firing is an act of unconscionable violence," he said. "*The New Yorker* has always been against violence, but now it is a part of it." A few people who wanted to leave with Bill found their reasons to leave. People who wanted to stay came up with their reasons to stay. Schell had a wife and three very young children, and he, like everyone else, needed the medical plan and the dental plan, not to mention the income. To Schell, these were not reasons to stay. Some of the staff people who stayed said that they were staying in order "to save the magazine," and they urged Jonathan Schell to stay, but he told them he could not go along with their rationalization.

Bill continued to worry about the life of the magazine. Newhouse would telephone him and ask for information relevant to Bill's practical, financial needs—the finances of the family; the cost of maintaining his daughter, Mary, in her special school; in whose name severance money should be designated. Bill didn't want to talk about any of it to Newhouse; he merely acceded to everything Newhouse suggested. Bill's mind was on the magazine. Bill told me he thought that I should leave the magazine, and I agreed. He told a few other staff members who were close to him that he thought that they should leave too, but they didn't want to leave. Some people reacted strangely. One woman came into Bill's office saying fervently, "I love you, Mr. Shawn! I love you!" But she didn't leave. Another writer came into my office, told me he was staying, tried to persuade me to stay, and said he would be guided by the words of James Joyce: *silence, exile,* and *cunning.* It was a disorienting time of heartbreak and craziness at *The New Yorker.*

In a way, Bill actually welcomed Newhouse's decision to fire him, to be relieved of the responsibility of his job. But Bill worried that the readers, the actual readers, would now abandon the magazine. He was disappointed and hurt, not by Mr. Newhouse's actions, but by the way his close friends behaved with him. After so many decades of giving so much to so many people, he had asked them for a token gesture of solidarity, and they had said no to him. He understood their "no." But he was being pictured erroneously by some of these same people as the man who didn't want to let go of them. The irony was that they wanted it both ways. They didn't want to let go of *him.* ("Nobody else can do what you can do.") However, he bent over backward with his friends, trying, as usual, to express what they seemed to be asking of him—his faith in their writing. He mourned, not for himself, not for McGrath, but for Mr. Newhouse. His affection for Newhouse was untouched; if anything, it was now increased. Every time he saw Si Newhouse, Bill told me, he saw one of those two little boys in their dark-blue suits coming into La Caravelle. (Actually, Si Newhouse, who was born in 1928, would have been in his thirties at the time. No matter. Whoever the boys were, to Bill the scene was unusually touching. To Bill, one of those boys would always be Si Newhouse.)

Clumsy as the firing was, Bill Shawn understood it, sympathized with it. For years, he had felt entrapped by his job but had not known how to free himself of it. He intimated some of that to Newhouse, who most likely was hardly equipped to understand the subtle, half-expressed equivocations and complexities of a man who felt he did not exist. But Bill genuinely wanted to help Mr. Newhouse and *The New Yorker.*

In 1986, the last year of Bill's editorship, he told me, the magazine made a profit of several million dollars. Its circulation was 560,070, an all-time high at that point. (*The New Yorker* started to lose money for the first time after Bill Shawn's departure, with losses mounting to $32 million by 1993. Under Tina Brown's leadership the losses, after six years, have declined dramatically.)

On his last day at the office, Bill wrote a letter to the staff. It was distributed to everyone in the office and also posted on the bulletin boards.

February 12, 1987

Dear colleagues, dear friends:

My feelings at this perplexed moment are too strong for farewells. I will miss you terribly, but I can be grateful to have had your companionship for part of my journey through the years. Whatever our individual roles at *The New Yorker,* whether on the eighteenth, nineteenth, or twentieth floor, we have built something quite wonderful together. Love has been the controlling emotion, and love is the essential word. We have done our work with honesty and love. *The New Yorker,* as a reader once said, has been the gentlest of magazines. Perhaps it has also been the greatest, but that matters far less. What matters most is that you and I, working together, taking strength from the inspiration that our first editor, Harold Ross, gave us, have tried constantly to find and say what is true. I must speak of love once more. I love all of you, and will love you as long as I live.

William Shawn

For forty-eight years, from the time Bill became managing editor in September 1939 until February 13, 1987, the day he left the magazine, he accumulated in his mind a set of what he called "principles," by which he felt he lived at *The New Yorker.* He called them "our principles." They were really his principles.

After Mr. Newhouse fired him, Bill wanted so much to explain the "principles" to the owner. He felt—optimistically—

that if he could explain what a terrible mistake it was to think in terms of editing a magazine for a "market," what a terrible mistake it was to be guided by "demographics," then Mr. Newhouse would understand and act accordingly. Bill was very hopeful when Mr. Newhouse agreed to meet with him. He really believed he had to try to tell Mr. Newhouse the truth about what makes a magazine great. In order to feel free of his responsibility for the lives of all the people involved with the magazine, as well as the life of the magazine itself, he truly believed, he had to explain how *The New Yorker* might survive. He couldn't abandon the magazine before he had done everything in his power to help it keep going. Then, and only then, could he be free of it.

Almost anyone hearing about Bill's eagerness would assume that what was on his mind was the hope that Mr. Newhouse would change his mind about the firing, but this was not what he was thinking about. On the day of Bill's appointment, I dropped him off, at the Carlyle, at four o'clock in the afternoon, Bill's favorite time of day. By five o'clock Bill joined me at home, looking crestfallen. "He was very impatient with me," Bill told me. "He really didn't want to hear what I was so eager to tell him, especially"—Bill gave a self-deprecating laugh—"the part about demographics. He *likes* demographics."

In early 1987, Bill and I were together more than ever. Erik was still in college. Roger Straus, of Farrar, Straus & Giroux, asked Bill to edit a few books, by writers who had written for *The New Yorker.* Straus wanted Bill to have his own imprint at Farrar, Straus. Bill refused, saying he believed that only two names belonged on a book—the publisher's and the author's. Straus wanted Bill to work at the FS&G offices. Bill agreed to edit a few books (including a book of brilliant *New Yorker* pieces about Europe by Jane Kramer), but he did not like the Farrar, Straus office, and almost immediately he decided not to work there. After editing the books he'd agreed to do, he did not want to go on with it. He would go to lunch with Straus and feel extremely sorry for the publisher and for everyone at Roger Straus's café, where, Bill said, he usually couldn't eat anything except toast.

Bill tried going to some local libraries to work, but he found them depressing. Mr. Newhouse had offered Bill an office at the Condé Nast building, but Bill didn't like the elevators there. Then Lorne Michaels, creator of *Saturday Night Live* on television, who had become a friend while I was doing a story about him, asked me if Bill had an office. When I said no, Michaels offered Bill the use of his own office at his company, Broadway Video, on the ninth floor of the Brill Building at 1619 Broadway. So Bill accepted Lorne Michaels's offer. There he enjoyed the company of the busy, cool, young entertainment makers, all of whom calmly took in stride the arrival among them of the courteous elderly gentleman. They didn't fuss over Bill, and he liked that. Every once in a while the people there would respectfully, and shyly, ask him an editorial question, and when he respectfully answered, they would be transported. Once, Cristina McGinniss, the office manager, asked Bill if he would edit her "mother's evaluation of her child" on her son's application to a nursery school. Bill complied in his inimitable way, and the application achieved its purpose.

We found ourselves working together at Broadway Video more and more. When Erik was in town, he would come to the office with us and help us graduate from the typewriter to the computer.

Bill had talked often about having the freedom to do some writing of his own, but now he was feeling the frustration of not being able to do it. He made several starts, but he cast them all aside. "I'm not writing what I wish to write," he would say. In his job as editor-in-chief, Bill had always enjoyed encouraging younger writers, and he was thrilled to discover the new or untried, especially if it was funny. At moments of discovery, he occasionally felt a pang of envy, but he would stifle it; he never permitted it to become full-fledged envy. The only piece of his writing published in *The New Yorker*—in the issue of November 14, 1936—was a story, "The Catastrophe." Cleanly written, unmistakably by him and with his humor, it was about a meteor landing "nice and tidy, on all five boroughs of Greater New York."

> Approximately seven and a half million New Yorkers, and over a half-million visitors from out of town (who cared very little for the city, anyway), had been annihilated. The only New Yorkers who escaped were corporations. Soon, too, the country was aware of a shortage of women's wear, advertising campaigns, international bankers, O. O. McIntyre. Conditions were, as analyzed by Roger W. Babson, unsettled.... there was a wave of Catastrophe jokes (Catastrophe who?), followed by a cycle of Catastrophe films.... People were getting bored with the whole subject.... It was not until the newspapers, in simultaneous spurts of fancy, decided to reprint the New York telephone directories as an obituary notice that the country began to grasp the scope and connotations of what had happened. New York City, like Pompei, was through.... Five years passed, and New York City had disappeared from the last map. Ten years passed, and it had taken on the aspect of a dim exaggeration. Twenty years, and there was a full generation without a single firsthand New York memory. Eventually, the few old-timers who still claimed to have seen New York were regarded as cranks. Nobody had the heart to tell them that New York had been invented by H. G. Wells.

The signature, characteristically, was only his initials, "W.S." He never again put his initials, let alone his name, on any writing of his other than letters.

CHAPTER 11

IN ORDER TO PROCEED

Bill would talk to me about his disappointment in the writing he attempted to do. More than anyone else in my experience, he had always been obsessed with death, but somehow, in our life together, both of us seemed to be trying to understand the meaning of life. I was impatient with most philosophizing about Life, but now I found myself thinking and feeling along with him. Neither one of us had been formally religious. There were no rituals we could look to for guidance. The poetry that I felt had always been latent in Bill might be the key to his finding some release in writing.

I seemed to be spending most of my time, my thoughts, and my feelings on Bill. I didn't question any of this. It seemed to me that it had to be this way. We caught up on movies and plays and concerts and museums. In 1988, Robin Williams and Steve Martin were onstage together, directed by Mike Nichols, in *Waiting for Godot,* at Lincoln Center Theater. After seeing the play, Bill and I went backstage, where Bill enjoyed a leisurely and serious discussion with Robin Williams about Samuel Beckett. The backstage environs were claustrophobic, which Bill didn't seem to mind at all. Bill and I were dividing our working time between home and the Broadway Video office. At home, he would often work sitting on our sofa, on his lap a nine-by-twelve-inch writing board, covered in Italian paper ("forget-me-not" was his favorite). He wrote on legal paper or plain white sheets with a ballpoint pen. At 1619 Broadway, he coped with his elevator problem by arranging with the elevator operators to go nonstop to the Broadway Video office on the ninth floor. Often, I would leave and go about my own business. On returning, if I found Bill in a state of frustration, we would talk about what he was trying to do. Gradually, we started working together. To get the writing flowing, we wrote a story for children. It was called "Blue" and was based on his experience as a child with a blue thread. A little boy has several encounters with the color blue—he is sent on an errand to buy blue thread, he gets lost in a blue pony cart, and so forth. Bill didn't want the story to be published. We worked on a couple of long stories, written in the first person singular, combining real memories with fiction. Bill didn't like it. "It is not what I wish to write," he would say. We decided it might be turned into a screenplay.

Bill Shawn never put his name on anything he worked on. If a name was necessary, we would invent one. "William LeFevre" was one. "David Hope" was another. We used "Lawrence LeFevre," for example, when Bill gave me a long and marvelous quote for my Talk story in 1967 about the Beatles' new (now historic) record "Sgt. Pepper's Lonely Hearts Club Band":

> This is really a coming of age for the Beatles. In musical substance, "Sgt. Pepper" is a much bigger advance than "Revolver," and "Revolver" was a tremendous advance, if you recall. There are many musical structures here that are both new and extremely interesting, as well as new combinations of rhythms, new chord progressions, new instrumentations,

> and a continuation of the great fresh flow of melody.... Many people have pointed out how eclectic the Beatles are. They've drawn on everything. But now this is *Beatles* music. Hundreds of people are imitating what they do, but no one even gets close. This record is a musical *event,* comparable to a notable new opera or symphonic work.... The Beatles write to please themselves. Unlike many artists now, who get their kicks out of offending the public, they're having a great time with the stuff itself. It has enormous cheerfulness, along with the sadness that keeps turning up. It's buoyant. This album is a whole world created by the Beatles. It's a musical comedy. It's a film. Only, it's a record.... Of course, you can't talk about the Beatles without mentioning the transcendent Duke Ellington. Just as he has never fit into the jazz scheme of things, the Beatles don't fit into the rock-'n'-roll scheme. They are off by themselves, doing their own thing, just as Ellington always has been. Like Ellington, they're unclassifiable musicians. And, again like Ellington, they are working in that special territory where entertainment slips over into art.

This quote by Bill, a. k. a. Lawrence LeFevre, in the Talk story elicited a tremendous response of appreciation from the Beatles themselves. Their manager telephoned to thank *The New Yorker* and said gratefully that no one had ever been able to identify the Beatles' art as "Lawrence LeFevre" had done. Hidden in my little Talk story, this was just one example of the way William Shawn hid his genius.

Some people saw Bill as submissive, but I saw him as genuinely meek, in the biblical sense. One day, he started talking about how he didn't wish to spend what little time he had left in his life on regret or bitterness. In my tribute to him published in *The New Yorker* right after his death, I quoted what he said: "I still have some bitterness, or at least disappointment, but I am trying to rid myself of it altogether: it serves no purpose, and it corrodes the soul.... I have never experienced, or

He felt he had to be the strong one, the infallible one, the one they knew they could count on.

even permitted myself to contemplate, a vindictive action. I would rather carry around pain or disappointment or even the residue of bitterness for the balance of my life than to entertain a moment's vengeful thought. In order to proceed, I have to shed the past. . . . Little bitterness remains, but that little is far too much for me. The truth is I cannot bear it. If I cannot love my enemies, I cannot breathe." I remembered how, years before, he had read to me the words of his beloved Dr. Cohn about "saintly people" having "an existence suspended in time."

A number of writers Bill had worked with wanted to continue to have his help, but then they found themselves in the embarrassing position of asking him to help them in work to be given to another editor. A few were not embarrassed, however. They seemed to take it for granted that they had a right to ask for Bill's help, and that it would be given. And it was. Others called him to inform him in detail about their various maladies—back problems, bone problems, diseases, operations, alcoholism, writer's block—and family illnesses and deaths. One writer with a malady, who had refused to sign the staff letter asking Gottlieb not to come for the job, regularly telephoned—Bill told me with an uncharacteristic sigh of impatience—to complain about Gottlieb's lack of sympathetic response to her.

Bill said he tried to do his best to offer these callers his interest in them, but it was a new time for him. He continued to worry about the talents of his writers and artists, but they were no longer available to him to hide his own talent in. He was losing interest in the individuals. Writers who wanted to continue working with him now seemed a burden to him. He made luncheon appointments with them and then canceled, feeling that he just could not take them on anymore.

Moreover, something internal was happening to Bill. He wanted time for himself. He didn't want to have to think about his former writers.

It wasn't much different with the bare handful of writers who had left the magazine with him. Bill managed to meet with Jonathan Schell several times to talk about a book Schell was writing about the Soviet Union. "I don't know what's the matter with me," Bill told me morosely. "It's difficult for me to feel any enthusiasm for any of this."

Many people outside *The New Yorker* also called him to say they were so sorry he wasn't going to edit the magazine anymore. Bill told me he was particularly surprised to have a call from Marlon Brando, whom he had never met. "He was very touching," Bill said.

As for myself, I found that I had come a long way from my "selfish young writer" days; I felt privileged to abandon the role of writer in relation to Bill. "You're different," one of the staff writers, a brilliant woman who stayed behind at the magazine, had said to me grimly when I told her I would not work for Gottlieb. "You're different because you can continue to have Bill Shawn as your editor any time you want him." I didn't know how to begin to tell her that Bill was, deep down, no more interested in my writing than he was in Jonathan Schell's, or for that matter in hers. Other writers who stayed behind and who still saw Bill for one reason or another continued to expect him to look forward to reading their work. They kept on telling him that they were still writing "for him." Hearing this made him self-conscious and uneasy, but he always read what was handed to him, and he tried, harder than ever, to respond with praise.

When he read an essay written by his daughter-in-law, Jamaica Kincaid, about her experience of growing up in Antigua, Bill was deeply affected by its literary force and was genuinely upset. "It's a poem of rage," he said to me. "It's a remarkable and powerful piece of writing," he said, shaking his head and repeating, "an unbelievable poem of rage."

But the writer whose work he now most looked forward to reading was his playwriting son Wallace. When Bill read his son's unique and heartfelt "The Fever"—a monologue read by Wallace (or by others) for audiences in theatres—he told me it was Wallace's most moving and impressive work.

I was just as happy not to be one of Bill's "staff writers" anymore. I was happy now just to be his friend, his ally, his lover, his partner, to help him, to see him exist, to exist with him.

Then it happened that we felt like writing together. We got the idea of doing a screenplay, putting other projects on hold for the time being. We did what neophyte screen writers do. We studied one of Syd Field's books about screenplay writing. In our minds, we started "seeing a movie" about the takeover of a magazine. We entitled our screenplay *Info.* It was the name of the fictional magazine in what we hoped would be our movie. We found it distracting and fun to work out the plot, delineate the characters, write the dialogue, and keep the action moving. We did a lot of laughing at our own efforts, laughing at the characters we were making, laughing at what we were creating out of our experiences with the real people at *The New Yorker.* Bill threw himself into the work with his old energy, concentration, and enthusiasm and was enjoying himself enormously. If he left, he would call me several times in the evening and read me bits of connecting dialogue he had written out; he would bring the new material along when he rejoined me. In making our characters, Bill wanted to make the "bad guys" much better than the real selves they were based on; he wanted to improve them, to make everybody "good."

The plot: *Info* is purchased by a billionaire, Max, who owns a lot of other magazines. He calls *Info* his "jewel in the crown." He wants it for his son, Ron, because it is "classy," and he hopes it will help give Ron more self-esteem. We had a high old time writing exchanges between Ron and Max.

RON: The worse *Info* is, the better it is for business.

MAX: There are worse things in the world than a good magazine. We can live with it.

At every succeeding birthday I had with him, he made me feel that the years were illusory but our love was real; our love was in what he called a "changeless" place.

We were having more fun than we'd had since the editing of *Picture.* Bill sat on our living-room sofa, a yellow legal pad on his lap, with his usual writing board for support, and scribbled dialogue after dialogue that we decided on together.

We sold the screenplay to a movie company. Today it is in the company's storehouse, along with scores of other unproduced screenplays.

So we had learned how to write a screenplay. Now we were ready to do another one. We quickly wrote a treatment and registered it with the Writers Guild. This one, called "The Knightly Virtues," was based on a chapter with that title in Robert Musil's *The Man Without Qualities,* one of Bill's favorite books.

A passage that set us off began: "Merkel had gone to Paris as a young man, some years before the First World War, and had never lost the imprint of those Paris years."

The characters in "The Knightly Virtues" bore a not inconsiderable resemblance to ourselves.

This one was going to be a wonderful and romantic movie. Bill and I could sense it. We both felt great. Every day, we couldn't wait to get to work on it. The more we wrote, the more we liked what we were doing. It was shaping up wonderfully. Bill was giving it his all. Our characters were strong, original, and exciting. Our story was dramatic, and we moved it along quickly. And it would take place in Paris. We took breathers from the work by going to the movies or heading for Central Park for walks.

One afternoon, while returning from the park, we saw Cecille, walking slowly, carrying packages. I felt a surge of affection for her that surprised me, and yet it felt totally natural. Bill held back with me. I found myself saying to him, "Go to her." It felt so natural, urging him to go over to her. But he still held back. "Go over to her," I heard myself saying. But he didn't go. We had been holding hands, and I found myself letting go of his hand. Without talking, we walked slowly back toward our apartment. I was thinking about how Bill used to stay with Cecille when she had the flu or other illness. That always felt right to me. Somehow, this meeting and his response felt wrong. Over four decades, I had absorbed Bill's feeling—or what I thought was his feeling—about his past and about her. He had, after all, asked me, on my European trip back in 1953, to retrace all their old Paris haunts.

"For God's sake, Bill, at this point along the line," I heard myself saying, "we all know what's happened. Why can't we just live, just *live*?"

He nodded in agreement. "It's too complicated," he said. "There's just too much I can't say. But it's all right," he added, clearly trying to reassure *me.*

Out of long habit, I accepted what he said without question.

"It's all right," he repeated.

We didn't say any more about it and returned to our apartment to work. There was no strain between us. We always talked freely to each other. I didn't have to ask him why I had urged him to go to her. But I asked myself—why *did* I feel that surge of affection? It was something I felt naturally, and that was that.

Bill's health had been good. In 1971, he had had what was called a mild heart attack, and he had been getting regular checkups with his cardiologist ever since. There was some doubt about whether he had had a genuine heart attack. It happened at a time when the magazine's publisher, in line with the "youth-crazed" obsessions of many other businesses, made retirement at age sixty-five mandatory for all staff people except William Shawn. Bill tried, without success, to fight the ruling, which affected the tireless, youthful William Maxwell, among others. Bill Shawn wanted every one of them to stay on. He believed then, and continued to believe, that age in years, for the most part, was meaningless. He knew, and tried to say, that with respect to creativity, some people still in their forties are old, and some people twice their age are young. He also had no self-conscious compunction about stating that he was neither old nor tired and that he worked harder than anyone else at the magazine. He believed passionately that creative people were usually ageless. He lost the argument. Some of his closest helpers were retired. Bill was devastated. He wound up in the hospital. When he came out, his cardiologist said he could find no damage to Bill's heart. In his latest checkup, his heart had been pronounced sound.

In 1987, Bill's humor was intact. His mind was as strong and as clear as ever. He was now eighty. His hearing was, to some slight extent, impaired, so with enormous disdain he consented to wear a hearing aid. He kept taking it off, saying "This thing is no damn good." Bill still hoped to get to writing some fiction of his own, but every time he thought about it, he said, he felt almost physically imprisoned. "There's just too much I am not free to say." That was the beginning and the end of it. But he was not giving up hope. In the meantime, he could have some fun with another screenplay, and at the very least, we could earn some money.

Then the unexpected hit. On Easter Day, 1992, he picked up a viral infection. He stayed in bed. He had had viral infections before, with a temperature, which he now had again. His internist, who lived in the Shawns' building, came to see him and prescribed an antibiotic and a tranquilizer. Bill telephoned me several times during that first day, each time trying to reassure me that he was all right, just weary, and the tranquilizer made him want to sleep. He made jokes about his "existence." He even made a joke about how he welcomed the virus, because now he could call off a lunch with somebody from out of town he didn't want to see. But I was frightened. For the next four days, when he called each morning, he sounded groggier than the day before. He was upset. He tried unsuccessfully to reach Wallace to ask him for help. For the first time, he felt he was losing control over his life. On the fifth day, he called later than usual, and his speech sounded slurred. Still, he called, as usual, every morning, and at the end of every day to say good night. However, he said that he was unsteady on his feet. He worried that he wasn't keeping accurate track of the number of tranquilizers he'd taken. I felt helpless and fearful. I tried to reach Wallace on the telephone and left messages with his answering service. I could not get through to him. Bill told me it was very difficult to reach Wallace, because he was in California looking for work as an actor.

After all these years of being together, convinced that I was deprived of "only one item on the list—a marriage certificate," I was finally discovering the power and the purpose of having that "one item."

Over the next several weeks, there were accidents of one kind or another. Bill suffered falls. One morning, Bill did not call. I called his special number. There was no answer. I called the regular number at the house. No answer to it, either. I was terribly frightened. I wanted to do something, but I didn't know what to do. I consulted with Erik, and we decided to wait it out for another twenty-four hours. Two days later, Bill finally called. His voice sounded strong and normal. He said that he had got out of bed two nights before and had fallen to the floor and couldn't get up. I was sick with worry. He was falling and hurting himself. I urged him to call his cardiologist, who asked him to come in to see him. After the visit, Bill sounded strong and clear. He was cheerful at the prospect of being able to consult his doctors. I went along with everything he told me. I was so accustomed to Bill's controlling his own life that I tried to take the events day by day and wait them out. Erik was home now and kept trying to reach Wallace on the telephone. No success. Erik left a long message with Wallace's answering service about obtaining some kind of watchful help for Bill, and about Bill's reaction to the sedatives and and about his injurious falls. Bill finally saw Wallace, and they talked about what they might do to improve the situation at home.

Eventually, Wallace called me. Wallace assured me that there was no serious danger to Bill's life. Then Wallace had to return to California. Bill visited his cardiologist again, and was given tests. Everything checked out O.K. By June, he was following a physical therapy routine programmed for him by the doctor, who said it was important for Bill to get back to his life and work. As a convenience, the cardiologist even picked up Bill in his car and brought him to his own home, where Erik and I were waiting to see him. Another doctor, a neurologist, made it possible for Bill to speak with him privately about his need to get out of the house. Bill's doctors were doing their best to help him regain control of his life. He now had a practical nurse, a pretty young Irish girl, to help him. He decided not to move for the summer to a rented house in Bronxville.

On August 31, Bill turned eighty-five. Wallace and Allen came to have a birthday dinner with him and Cecille. I sent over thirty-one yellow tea roses. Bill really seemed to be on his way back to good health. We both had talked eagerly that morning about resuming the full pattern of our life together. In the middle of the dinner, Bill told me, Cecille said she felt ill. So Bill, Wallace, and Allen took her to the hospital, where she stayed for a week and had a battery of tests, after which the doctors said they could find nothing wrong with her and released her. Bill told me that Wallace and Allen were doing a lot of talking with him about how to improve his situation all around.

Bill continued his therapy sessions to build up his strength. Tina Brown, who was just under forty, was now the new editor-in-chief of *The New Yorker.* Bill tended to dismiss gossipy criticisms of anyone, including her, and always looked for what might really be there. He took her seriously and planned to see her right after Thanksgiving to discuss working with her as a consultant. He had never fully stopped looking at *The New Yorker*, but now he was reading it with new interest. The day before Thanksgiving, Erik and I were to have dinner with Bill at La Caravelle, to celebrate his getting back to work. He was feeling and looking much better. Bill was excited about the prospect of a festive evening. He was going to pick up Erik at home, and both of them would meet me at the restaurant. We were going to celebrate. I had the feeling that we were going to celebrate our life, his existence with me. But it turned out to be impossible for Bill to have the dinner. Looking distraught, he came to the restaurant with Erik and said he had to go right back to his apartment uptown.

By then, Bill had asked me if I would go to see his cardiologist and his neurologist to ask them what I might do to help. So I did that. Both doctors were extremely sympathetic and understanding, and they said that they would try to help. They did indeed help. The cardiologist told me that in his last examination of Bill, he had found him improved. Bill had come to see him feeling very despondent and discouraged. "When I told him that he was improving and would continue to improve, he perked up," the doctor told me. "He suddenly stood straighter and taller."

Bill was still getting calls from people who wanted one thing or another. He wrote notes in response, and he continued to worry, as he had always done, about not hurting feelings. He got into the habit of reading some of his notes to me on the telephone, to be sure that his responses were, he said, "adequate." In the last few days of his life, he read me a note he had just written to William Buckley, thanking him for sending him a copy of his "lovely new book." Bill wanted to be sure he sounded "enthusiastic." Sometimes in the early evening he would be driven half a mile to the south in order to be with

Erik and me. Early one Friday night the three of us met for supper at the EAT restaurant on Madison Avenue. Bill was, for the moment, free and in charge of his life. His interest in his existence flickered. He was not giving up. We talked about Erik's acceptance at a graduate school to study for a master's degree in environmental studies. Then Bill edited the copy for the cover of a forthcoming paperback edition of my book *Picture.* As I wrote in a memorial tribute to him in *The New Yorker:* "With his pencil, he made his characteristically neat proofreading marks on a sentence that said the book 'remains as fresh and unique as ever.' He changed it to read 'remains unique and as fresh as ever.' He said to us: 'There are no degrees of uniqueness.' He was the one to know that. He embodied the meaning of the word. Later, I looked up, in *The Concise Oxford Dictionary,* the definition of 'unique': 'a. of which there is only one, unequalled, having no like or equal or parallel.' "

That day, Erik and I had gone to Brooks Brothers and bought Bill a new dark-blue suit with a white pinstripe (38 short) and had brought it with us to the restaurant. Bill tried on the jacket. It fit perfectly. He planned to wear the new suit to a lunch with Tina Brown. When we walked outside with him to his car, I noticed that his eyes, strangely and frighteningly, were no longer blue. They had become black, deep black.

This phenomenon was chilling, but there had been hundreds of disturbances that Bill had had to face alone over our years together, and I tried not to give this one special significance. Bill wouldn't stop fighting for his life, would he? During his illness, he had seemed to give up control over his life; now there was this surge to regain that control. The flow of our life had been forcibly changed. Would he fight for it? Or would he submit? Impossible. I pushed aside the questions that were imposing themselves upon me. He couldn't possibly stop fighting for his life. After all, he had tried on the new suit.

Erik and I had made an appointment with a tailor at Brooks Brothers to have the pants of Bill's new suit fitted four days later, a Tuesday. That Monday evening we said good night, as we had every night for over four decades. The next morning, I dialed his number as usual. For the only time in our long life together, his wife answered the telephone.

"He's gone," she said, as soon as she heard my voice. "He's gone," she repeated.

Erik and I rushed out and took a taxi half a mile north, arriving in about three minutes. We went directly up to the apartment on the second floor and knocked. Wallace, now a balding man in his late forties, came to the door and held it slightly ajar when he saw us. He was in shock, afraid to admit us. He looked behind him, to his mother, for permission.

"Let them in," she said.

On some impulse, I embraced her.

"He died in my arms," she said.

On that grievous morning, Erik and I put our mouths in farewell to Bill's cold forehead. Erik and I, bending mournfully over him, felt fear, his kind of fear. We both took on the fear as a kind of comfort. It would be a constant reminder to us of Bill's view of every life as fragile and sacred, to be protected from hurt and violence, and to be filled, whenever possible, with gaiety and fun.

As a small child, I witnessed fragility in the helpless form of my baby brother, Teddy. Bill, with his longing for life, somehow knew how to get beyond helplessness. He knew what he was asking me to do with my life. I went to him because it was life for both of us. In every possible way, he filled my life with the protection and with the love he promised.

I hear these days, from so many confident, watchful, attractive young women, who are so much more sophisticated than I was at their age, about the rules that have arisen in response to the unacceptable patterns of behavior of some men and women in the workplace. I have enormous respect and admiration for most of these smart young women. When I wonder, occasionally, what they might have done in my place forty-five years ago, I get lost in uncertainty about them. But I am sure always—always—that I would do again exactly what I did do then. What's more, I think that Bill would do the same. I'm sure he would be proud to read this story. Today I find nothing to regret in the course I chose to follow with Bill. I was part of his living. He always made it clear to me that he could never abandon Cecille. He told me of his love for, and his pride in, his children, and he shared with me the details of their happy experiences with each other. He kept me thoroughly posted on their growing up. So today, I continue, very naturally, to have feelings of sympathy and friendship for his entire family.

He had said to me that both of us, in the beginning, were innocents, and neither of us knew the unforeseen and difficult terrain we were heading into. We may have been inexperienced, but both of us knew from the start that we were setting out to create our life in an untried way. We seemed to go along with the confidence that love bestows upon innocents. It was Bill who kept it, for the most part, from becoming truly difficult.

Today, as I go out to report one of my little "Talk of the Town" stories, or as I undertake a longer piece of writing, I start out, invariably, smiling and, invariably, I am thinking of Bill. He is always in me. If I am writing something funny, his wistful, eager, appreciative response is part of me. It's because of Bill, I'm sure, that I still am not tired of this work, and I am never bored. It remains fun for me. My son, Erik, is now on his own—a qualified environmentalist—and he's a sharp reader.

I've never been impelled to write anything "big," anything "ambitious." Making Bill laugh was the entire bag of tricks for me. It remains so to this day. I was able to write "The Shit-

Kickers of Madison Avenue"—a funny and moving story about fifteen-year-old private schoolers on New York's Upper East Side—because they accepted me, without condescension, and openly gave me their precious, rhythmic talk. It was three years after Bill died, and I could feel his delight in them. I could *feel* it.

Beyond the writing, I am constantly aware of Bill's presence, in whatever I do, wherever I go. It was in his nature to have a voice that did not rise, a touch that was gentle, and a will to forgive. He tried to give life to everyone in every way as best he could, and until that moment, after our final supper, when I saw his eyes go black, he always held on to the hope that he would have life for himself. As I look around, in every minuscule motion on the streets and in the parks, in the shops and in the gyms, among the busboys and among the bus drivers, in the flimflams and in the screw-ups, in the "zooed" and "zonk" jargoned disciples of my son Erik's age, in every place and in every way and with anyone, I'm always seeing what Bill would see and how he would see it. And when I look at Erik, who absorbed so much of Bill's kindness and spirit and grace, I know, that he, too, will always have Bill as his guide.

To the world, William Shawn was known as the great editor, but in essence he was a poet. He created poems for me at odd moments, even while we rode in a taxi on the way to our office. His poems were often about the cherished fragments of the love and warmth he had longed for and was able to find in his life. He liked to think about a little jazz combo playing on after he was gone, and of books that would still be read long after he was dead.

"Our time together defied death," Bill had said to me. Every day, I am able to look out at the world with all the joy and laughter and life he put into me, and so I'm able to find joy and laughter and life always and know we are still together, defying death.

ILLUSTRATION CREDITS

Pages 18 (top left), 136 (top), 139 (bottom): William Shawn
Page 24: Henry Grossman
Page 41 (bottom): Simeon Ross
Page 67: Mary Hemingway
Pages 92 (bottom), 95 (top): Silvia Reinhardt
Page 95 (bottom): Arthur Freed
Page 96 (top): Oona Chaplin
Page 182 (bottom): James Ivory
Page 206: Penelope Gilliatt
Pages 13, 41 (top), 96 (bottom), 120 (top), 127, 230:
photographer unknown
All other photographs by Lillian Ross

Drawing page 32: Abe Birnbaum

ABOUT THE AUTHOR

LILLIAN ROSS was born in Syracuse, New York. She worked as a staff writer at *The New Yorker* from 1945 until 1987 and returned to the magazine in 1993. Ms. Ross is the author of eleven books, including *Picture, Portrait of Hemingway, Moments with Chaplin, The Player* (with her sister, Helen Ross), *Vertical and Horizontal, Talk Stories, Takes,* and *Reporting.*

ABOUT THE TYPE

The text of this book was set in Janson, a misnamed typeface designed in about 1690 by Nicholas Kis, a Hungarian in Amsterdam. In 1919 the matrices became the property of the Stempel Foundry in Frankfurt. It is an old-style book face of excellent clarity and sharpness. Janson serifs are concave and splayed; the contrast between thick and thin strokes is marked.